THE WAY OF
THE HUNTER-WARRIOR

THE WAY
OF THE
HUNTER-WARRIOR

*How To Make a Killing
In Any Market*

Julian M. Snyder

RICHARDSON & SNYDER BOOKS
1982

Copyright © 1982
BIRKDALE TRADING INTERNATIONAL S.A.

Snyder, Julian
The Way of the Hunter-Warrior

LIBRARY OF CONGRESS
CATALOGING IN PUBLICATION DATA

1. Anthropology – Pre-history – 11th Century
2. Investment – U.S.
3. Samurai Tradition

Julian M. Snyder, Author
Hardbound
ISBN 0-943940-00-1

LIBRARY OF CONGRESS CATALOG NUMBER 82-61459

Manufactured in the United States of America
COVER DESIGN: Lawrence Ratzkin

ACKNOWLEDGEMENTS

Ardrey, Robert, *The Hunting Hypothesis.* New York: Atheneum Publishers, 1976. Brown, Norman O., *Life Against Death.* Middletown, Conn.: Wesleyan University Press, 1957. Castaneda, Carlos, *Journey to Ixtlan.* New York: Pocket Books, 1972. Castaneda, Carlos, *A Separate Reality.* New York: Simon & Schuster, 1971. Davies, Trevor R., *The Golden Century of Spain.* Houndsmills, England: MacMillian Press Ltd., 1937. Gray, J. Glenn, *The Warriors, Reflection on Men in Battle.* New York: Harper & Row, 1977. Georgescu-Roegen, Nicholas, *The Entrophy Law and the Process of Economics.* Cambridge, Mass.: Harvard University Press, 1971. Groseclose, Elgin, *Money and Man,* Fredrick Ungar Publishing Company, 1961. Keith, Elmer, *Guns and Ammo for Hunting Big Game.* Los Angeles: Peterson Publishing Company, 1965. Mishima, Yukio, *The Way of the Samurai,* translated by Kathryn Sparling. New York: Basic Books, Inc., 1977. Mitchell, Wesley, *History of the Greenbacks,* 2nd ed., Chicago: The University of Chicago Press, 1968. Musashi, Miyamoto, *A Book of Five Rings.* Translated by Victor Harris. Woodstock, New York: The Overlook Press, 1974. Ortega y Gasset, José, *Meditations on Hunting.* Translated by Howard B. Wiscott. New York: Charles Scribner's Sons, 1972. Smith, William Lord, *"Hunting Dangerous Game," Handbook of Travel.* Cambridge, Mass.: Harvard University Press, 1935. Sumner, William Graham, *The Financer and the Finances of the American Revolution,* 2 vols., New York: Augustus M. Kelly Publisher, 1896. Tsunetomo, Yamamoto, *Hagakure: The Book of the Samurai,* Translated by William Wilson, New York: Kodansha International Ltd., 1979. Tsunetomo, Yamamoto, *Hagakure: A Code to the Way of the Samurai.* Translated by Takao Mukoh, Japan: Hokuseido Press, 1980. Washburn, S.L. and Avis, Virginia, *Behavior and Evolution.* Edited by Anne Roe and George Gaylord Simpson, New Haven, Conn.: Yale University Press, 1958. Vacca, Roberto, *The Coming Dark Age.* Translated by J.S. Whale, Garden City, New York: Doubleday, 1973.

for
Tiger Kim

CONTENTS

THE WAY OF
THE HUNTER-WARRIOR

INTRODUCTION

It was a cold autumn day in Paris in 1977. Several inches of snow lay on the streets outside the Ritz where I had, supported by the last of my pocket cash, taken a suite—there being no single or double rooms available there or at any of the cheaper hotels where I was used to staying when I was in the City of Light.

I was in my room. I had just come from Basle, Switzerland where I had met privately with Rene Larre, General Manager of the Bank for International Settlements. The outcome of our conversation was that the U.S. dollar looked weak and could perhaps grow weaker—possibly even crash—and I was writing about this for the next issue of International MONEYLINE. I had been writing all night and as dawn lightened the Paris rooftops, my conviction that the dollar would fall and the Swiss franc rise, grew. I called New York and dictated my newsletter. Then, on an impulse, I called my broker, Phil Nash, at Conti Commodities in New York.

"How's the franc?"

"Looks weak," he said, giving me the quote on the International Monetary Market in Chicago. My stomach turned over; was I wrong? But I heard my voice saying, "Buy one. Buy March."

"Buy one?" Phil sounded incredulous.

Exhaustion from the night's work came over me. International MONEYLINE had been losing money for months. I had no money to trade with—only enough to survive for about another thirty days. I could clearly see the end of my newsletter adventures, my trading, my confidence in all I knew, looming in front of me. But suddenly I was no longer concerned. I was calm, indifferent to my fate, almost even amused. As I became aware of the sunlight slicing through the half-shuttered windows like a sword of light, a phrase from the Japanese samurai came into my mind: **Ai Uchi!** (Cut your opponent before he cuts you).

"Buy five. No, buy ten. No, make it 20 contracts, Swiss francs (value–$1,250,000)," I told Phil. I knew he would take the order, and I also knew I did not have the margin to cover my purchases. In the samurai tradition, faced by a crisis, I had chosen death—or, in this case, financial suicide.

An hour or so later, a call from my secretary confirmed the worst. The franc apparently had gone down. I was wiped out financially.

I went for a walk in the snow and bought a silk scarf at Pierre Balmain (I still have it). Then I returned to the Ritz, called some friends, ordered some champagne and had a party.

Three hours later there was another call from the U.S.

Amazing news: I had been given the wrong quote; December, instead of March. I had not been wiped out after all. Instead, I was ahead by about $25,000. The party continued on a new note. I had risked everything and won. My business had been saved at a stroke by a decision "from the void." It was a feeling I had had once during a karate tournament in New York: Shikan-Tazza, the heightened state of awareness in Zen associated with "the way of the warrior." In those last moments when I gave the order on the telephone, I knew I had experienced something unusual. . . .

And this is what this book is about: an almost completely forgotten tradition, a tradition that may stretch back 10 or 20 million years, a tradition that can help you—as it helped me—learn to follow the way of the hunter-warrior in investing and trading in financial markets.

However, to find this path, first some history must be rewritten.

I

THE RETURN OF THE HUNTER-WARRIOR

While we are members of the intelligent primate family, we are uniquely human in the noblest sense, because for untold millions of years we alone killed for a living.
Robert Ardrey, *The Hunting Hypothesis*

IN WAYS THAT PEOPLE
have largely forgotten, mankind is superbly equipped for survival by millions of years of evolution. Jean-Jacques Rousseau, who thought that man in his primal state was happy, amiable and good and Charles Darwin, who believed that our ancestors were placid vegetarian apes, both have been proven wrong by more recent discoveries. A two-volume social history of man puts it this way:

> The most important influence in man's cultural and evolutionary history is his long existence as a hunter of wild animals.

Yet much of the current sentiment against guns and hunting has obscured the fact that man has always been a hunter.

Not until 1925 did anyone suggest that early man was a predatory being, when Professor Carveth Read, of the University of London, published his *Origins of Man,* in which he suggested that our earliest ancestors ate meat and hunted game in large packs. At about the same time, Raymond A. Dart discovered the remains of a human creature in South Africa which he named "Australopithecus." In 1953 he published his paper, "The Predatory Transformation from Ape to Man," which cited evidence to show that the australopithecines were not only meat eaters, but armed hunters. So began a revolution in anthropology. In 1956, one of

America's most noted anthropologists, Professor S. L. Washburn of the University of California at Berkley advanced further arguments for Robert Ardrey's *The Hunting Hypothesis*:

> Man is man, and not a chimpanzee because, for millions of evolving years, we killed for a living.

More broadly stated, Ardrey says:

> . . . if among all the members of our primate family the human being is unique, even in our noblest aspiration, because we alone through untold millions of years were continuously dependent on killing to survive.

In a 1956 symposium at Princeton, Professor Washburn said:

> Hunting not only necessitated new activities and new kinds of cooperation, but changed the role of the adult male in the group. Among the vegetable primates, adult males do not share food. They take the best places for feeding and may even take food from less dominant animals. However, since sharing the kill is normal behavior for many carnivores, economic responsibility of the adult males and the practice of sharing food in the group probably resulted from being carnivorous. The very same actions that caused man to be feared by other animals led to food-sharing, more cooperation, and economic interdependence.
>
> The world view of early human carnivore must have been very different from his vegetarian cousins. The desire for meat leads animals to know a wider range and to learn the habits of many animals. Human territorial habits and psychology are fundamentally different from those of apes and monkeys.

Not only does man's habit of sharing food put him in the company of the carnivores, but the entire evolution of the family life style is consistent with the hunting way of life. In other words, the man went out hunting while the woman stayed at home and took care of the slow-to-mature children, who needed constant attention. Man's capacity to organize and cooperate also correlates with the ancient hunting band which, interestingly enough, was usually composed of 10 to 12 men, about the size of a modern football team, jury, or corporate board of directors. Radiogenic methods of dating were able to trace the hunting hominid through fossils, back more than 5 million years with the possibility that manlike creatures had operated in hunting bands on this planet for as long as 20 million years. This is an eternity of time compared to the mere 10 thousand years that man has been a grower of wheat, barley and beans and keeper of such animals as goats, sheep and cattle.

You have often heard the observation that a nuclear war would send the survivors back to the Stone Age. I don't agree that thermonuclear war is inevitable, and that if it happened a backward journey would follow. Yet, it's useful to speculate what life in the Stone Age would be like.

You are living in what is now southern Europe, some 75,000 years ago. It is early spring and traces of snow are still on high ground. You are a member of a band of thirty people who live in a cave near what is now the Mediterranean Sea. Your group needs about 600 pounds of fresh meat each week to live well. You can, and have, subsisted on less, but you also ate roots and pulverized tree bark and nuts. If you are a man, you are part of a hunting party that has been going out for fresh meat almost every day for as long as you can remember. You have never worried about the hunt; it's second nature to you. Your thoughts are on how the animals will be trapped or killed—the particular tactics you're going to use. The eventual success of the hunt is beyond question. Only the particular technique suited to the quarry, the terrain, and the weather are on your mind.

In the morning, meat is cooked over a fire in front of your cave by one of the women in the group. After eating, you and the rest of the hunting party wrap yourselves in furs and skins and, carrying stone axes, knives and wooden spears, leave the cave area in search of game. The party separates into five pairs in order to cover as much territory as possible. In this part of the world you may find reindeer, wild horses, elephants, goats and even huge cave bears. While the hunting party is away, the women left behind look after the children, scrape animal skins for clothing and search for rabbits or other small game. Several of the women are expert at catching fish in the nearby sea.

The hunting party—a hundred yards between each two-man team—has covered two or three miles before one of the pairs sees the tracks and fresh feces of a reindeer herd. The animals cannot be far away and the hunters move forward slowly, silently, trying to stay upwind of the pack.

The reindeer are gathered on the shore of a small lake grazing on grass and lichen. There is still a thin film of ice on the water, but it will not support the animals. Beyond the reindeer herd, the vegetation indicates that the ground is soft and almost marshy. Signaling each other by striking stones together, half of the hunting party has gathered just behind the crest of a hill overlooking the lake and the feeding animals. They decide to stampede the reindeer into the bog so that one or more of them will be slowed enough to kill.

Ideally, the stampede would be started with torches, but the fire is at the cave and it would take too long to go and get it.

The hunters decide to try stampeding the reindeer by surprise, aware that some of the bucks may charge them instead of running away. At a signal, the hunting party on the hill stands up and runs down toward the reindeer, screaming and waving their spears and axes. They are lucky. The reindeer panic and flee. In the open, they can run at thirty miles an hour. But, running across the bog they move much slower, and an older buck gets a leg stuck in a particularly soft place. At once, the hunters are upon him, thrusting with their spears. The reindeer is still strong and dangerous, but they kill him in a few minutes.

Meanwhile, the other half of the hunting party has lain in wait on the other side of the bog to ambush the frightened herd in flight. They are lucky, too. One of the hunters manages to hurl his spear deep into the flank of a fleeing reindeer. The wound slows the animal and the spear thrower's companions run after it. The chase takes the group more than a mile, but at last, in a thicket of saplings, the hunters catch up and find the reindeer down on its forelegs. Dodging the animal's antlers, several of the men use their spears on the reindeer until it is dead.

A pair of the hunters runs back to the cave to bring butchering knives and women to help with the job. While they are gone, some of the hunters fashion knives from stones near the lake and begin. By nightfall, the hunting party is back at their cave with enough meat, organs and marrow-filled bones to last for a week. The group builds up the fire and gorges themselves. Outside in the night, a hyena calls. By the new moon the weather will be warmer and you know that the hunting will be easier.

Modern life as it has evolved may not require hunting-related instincts and there may be sound reasons for women to seek equality and for all peoples to live in peace. However, in attempting to reach such goals, we may be fighting the evolution of a million generations as compared to a mere 500 generations since the dawn of recorded history. It is even possible that the very qualities which most of us condemn in ourselves—aggression and cruelty—may have evolved from the same basic society that produced compassion and mercy. As Ardrey points out:

> No human inventory can fail to include our propensity for premeditated organized murder of our fellows yet fails to note that an army is a model of cooperation and self-sacrifice, or that no other species carefully, tenderly cares for its wounded, even for its enemies.

Whether or not the above assertions are as spectacularly true as they appear, it should be obvious that the hunting approach to life—whether or not anything is actually hunted—is a natural part of our heritage, and is certainly a key to survival, even in the concrete jungles and rubbish-strewn alleys of the world. There are striking similarities between the hunting or warrior philosophies of the ancient Greeks, the Japanese samurai and the American Indian—similarities which can be applied successfully not only to the hunting of wild animals (and even men) but to that most dangerous game of modern industrial society: the hunt for money.

Interestingly enough, the real hunter-warrior, who is stereotypically thought of as a killer-destroyer, unlike the industrial leader, who shows little concern over polluting his environment, respects his game and leaves nature in ecological balance. For instance, in *Journey to Ixtlan,* Carlos Casta-neda declares that the hunter touches the world around him-self sparingly:

> You don't eat five quail, you eat one. You don't damage the plants just to make a barbeque pit. You don't expose yourself to the power of the wind unless it is mandatory. You don't use people until they have shrivelled to nothing, especially the people you love.

The hunter is "not squeezing his world out of shape," says Castaneda's Don Juan, "he taps it lightly, stays for as long as he needs to and then lightly slips away leaving hardly a mark." This is a far cry from the great scars on our Western mountains left by the strip miners of coal and the open-pit miners of copper. The hunter's attitude is also quite removed from the fear and greed which clichéd commentary always identifies as the principal sociological polarities of the marketplace.

> A hunter knows he will lure game into his trap over and over again. To worry is to become unwittingly accessible. And once you worry you cling to anything out of desperation, once you cling you're bound to get exhausted and then you exhaust whoever or whatever you are clinging to.

In the stock market or in commodities markets, the suc-cessful professional trader does not cling desperately to his investment position; if he sees he is wrong, he cuts his losses. If he sees he has a good profit in a short period of time, he takes his profit calmly, without greedily reaching for the last dollar. One of the most successful money hunters of the 19th century, who singly built the Rothschild fortune said: "I always buy too late and sell too soon."

In contrast, the average person displays toward an investment the kind of nervous exhaustion that is called "buck fever" among deer hunters. Buck fever is the nervous trembling of the arms and hands that causes a hunter to miss an easy shot. The hunter sees the deer clearly in the sight of his rifle, but he has become too anxious, he has thought about this moment too much, he has planned for it too long, he has lost sleep over it and now, when the kill is surely his, he misses the shot.

The stereotype of the modern hunter is that of the pointless killer, and there are admittedly some of these around. However, their attitudes are more often reflections of the points of view of the trained corporate manager or bureaucratic killer out on a spree, than those of the hunter of the vast prehistory of this planet.

As José Ortega y Gasset points out in his prescient book, *Meditations on Hunting,* for hundreds of years of recorded history, hunting was considered to be the primary pleasure of the aristocrat or so-called liberated man who could do whatever he liked. In addition, Ortega notes:

> this greatly liberated man, the aristocrat has always done the same things: raced horses or competed in physical exercises, gathered at parties where the feature is dancing, and engaged in conversation. But, before any of those and consistently more important . . . he has been hunting.

As opposed to these avocations, Ortega y Gasset notes:

> The fact is that for almost all men the major part of life consists of obligatory occupations, chores which they would never do out of choice. Since this fate is so ancient and so constant, it would seem that man should have learned to adapt

himself to it and consequently to find it charming. But he does not seem to have done so. Although the constancy of the annoyance has hardened us a little, these occupations imposed by necessity continue to be difficult. They weigh upon our existence, mangling it, crushing it. In English such tasks are called "jobs"; in the Roman languages the term for them derived from the Latin word *trepalitum*, which originally meant a terrible torture.

However, the pleasure of the hunt, whether for game or for money, is rarely really relaxing. As Ortega says:

Hunting, like all human occupations, has its different levels, and how little of the real work of hunting is suggested in words like diversion, relaxation, entertainment! A good hunter's way of hunting is a hard job which demands much from man: he must keep himself fit, face extreme fatigues, accept danger. It involves a complete code of ethics of the most distinguished design; the hunter who accepts the sporting code of ethics keeps his commandments in the greatest solitude with no witnesses or audience other than the sharp peaks of the mountain, the roaming cloud, the stern oak, the trembling juniper, and the passing animal. In this way, hunting resembles the monastic rule and the military order. So, in my presentation of it as what it is, as a form of happiness, I have avoided calling it pleasure. Doubtless in all happiness there is pleasure, but pleasure is the least of happiness.

Modern man seeks money as a symbol of immortality and when it loses value he feels vulnerable. Yet running throughout the hunter-warrior philosophies of ancient Japan and Greece is a basic contempt for death. To live, to survive and yes, even to be happy, you do not need a religion, a bank account or a government to take care of you. You need only faith in yourself. For example, in *Hidden Leaves*, a book writ-

31

ten in the 17th century, Yamamoto Tsunenori describes the fundamental attitude of the warrior as being the resolute acceptance of death:

> There is no way to describe what a warrior should do other than that he should adhere to the Way of the warrior (Bushido). I find that all men are negligent of this. There are few men who can quickly reply to the question "What is the Way of the warrior?" This is because they do not know in their hearts. From this we can see that they do not follow the Way of the warrior. By the Way of the warrior is meant death. The Way of the warrior is death. This means choosing death whenever there is a choice between life and death. It means nothing more than this. It means to see things through, being resolved. . . . If you keep your spirit correct from morning to night, accustomed to the idea of death and resolved on death, and consider yourself as a dead body, thus becoming one with the Way of the warrior, you can pass through life with no possibility of failure and perform your office properly.

Or, as Don Juan says in Carlos Castaneda's *A Separate Reality:*

> The spirit of the warrior is not geared to indulging or complaining or in winning or losing. The spirit of the warrior is geared only to struggle and every struggle is the warrior's last battle on earth . . . and as he wages his battle knowing that his will is impeccable, a warrior laughs and laughs.

This last quotation has a very special meaning for me. A successful stock-market speculator in the late 1960s, I had savored the "good life" in Beverly Hills and then retired to spend my time studying and traveling in Europe and Canada. But by 1973, I was out of money. My economic studies told me that we were moving rapidly into a period of double-digit inflation, when the price of gold and other precious metals would skyrocket, but I had no funds with which to take advantage of my projections.

With an investment of only $700, I started a financial newsletter called International MONEYLINE to tell people about the coming inflation. My first mailing produced only 8 subscribers, but I did not give up. In my notebook on financial markets and economic developments, I had scrawled, "this is my last battle on earth." I made money from the newsletter (circulation currently 18,000) and from my investments, but by the middle of 1976, the decreasing rate of inflation and the decreasing price of gold, even though I had accurately forecast it, began pushing me toward what seemed to be an inevitable failure.

I had been studying the Oriental martial arts during this period, and reading *A Book of Five Rings* by Miyamoto Musashi, the 16th century sword-saint of Japan who advocated "choosing death" in difficult combat situations. For me, death lurked in the wildly fluctuating currency and commodity markets where, with inadequate financial reserves, an individual could be wiped out in an afternoon. Nevertheless, as I described, I went into the currency markets with all my limited financial resources, and bought forward contracts in the Swiss franc. The franc made an immediate rise and following my initial play, I began to trade heavily and dangerously, but with an inner calm that I had never known before. I was on what Sun Tzu, the Chinese general who wrote on the art of war 2,000 years ago, called "death ground": "ground in which the army survives only if it fights with the courage of desperation." As Sun Tzu explained it:

> Let the troops do their tasks without imparting your designs;
> use them to gain advantage without revealing the dangers in-

volved. Throw them into a perilous situation and they survive; put them in death ground and they will live.

In 1978, I alternated between my trading room on Broad
Street in Manhattan and the karate studio of Tiger Kim, in the
Bronx, attempting to follow the way of the warrior, both
physically and financially. I made better than 100 percent
profits for both myself and my increasing clients, as the circulation of International MONEYLINE grew, becoming a mil-
lionaire in the process, and I began to see clearly the remarkable connection between ancient hunter-warrior strategies
and modern money hunting and financial survival.

The attitude of the hunter-warrior and the incredible coolness exhibited in times of stress by the most successful financial operators, I realized, are one and the same. But the meaning really goes deeper. We are talking not so much about
combat, death or the making of money but, in reality, an attitude toward life itself.

Millions of years of natural selection have produced
modern man. He is uniformly descended from successful
hunters. Those of our ancestors who were not skilled at the
hunt, probably made a mistake and were killed. We have
spent the past 8,000–10,000 years laying a veneer of civilization over our primitive hunting instincts, but He, the Hunter,
still exists in all of us—a historic archetype waiting to be re-
leased. He comes out when we least expect it. When danger
threatens, the adrenaline flows automatically, and we are
ready for fight or flight, regardless of the thousands of years
of training designed to repress these feelings. The Hunter
comes out when we are in battle, whether it is for life or for
prestige in the schoolyard. He comes out in the violence of
contact sports. He surfaces in sexual excitement and—most

important—the Hunter is at work in the attitudes of most highly successful businessmen and investors.

The problem with our hunter instinct is to know when to let Him out and when to put Him back in the cave of our mind. Without understanding your hunter and being able to call on him at will, you will not survive. Unfortunately, most of us have been taught that the Hunter is wicked, that he represents impulses that need to be suppressed and controlled. The same sort of teaching often affects people's attitudes toward money and investing. To act as a Hunter in the market is to offend the delicate sensibilities of people whose morality and ideas of how things ought to be constantly get in the way of how and what they buy and sell.

II

BECOMING A FINANCIAL SAMURAI

In hunting dangerous game the most effective weapon is one's own fortitude. Oftentimes, the contest between man and beast is decided before a shot is fired, and the stronger personality wins. Given a natural instinct for hunting, the best battery of rifles in the world . . . these advantages will avail little unless a crisis precipitates you into an unbeatable attitude of mind. It is common for the mind to become chaotic and the nerves loose-jointed just before coming to shot [sic]. When you bring up your rifle this chaos must crystallize immediately into staunch material. Your survival instincts clear your head and act for you. There is little time to think. The thinking must be done in camp. . . . Constant thoughts of safety are dangerous. . . .

William Lord Smith
Hunting Dangerous Game

Hunting Big Game

involves going against the cautious and apprehensive style with which most of us approach life. Hunting, like auto racing or skydiving, is a dangerous sport and a good part of the attraction is the lure of danger. It offers an excitement that psychologists call a "peak experience"—the feeling of being totally alive, mind and body in tune and at one with nature. This feeling is not often felt in the workaday world where we function bound by ceremony and rules of proper behavior. The desire for a peak experience is one of the reasons for the enormous boom in spectator sports and the wide popularity of adventure books and movies. As Thoreau said, "The mass of men lead lives of quiet desperation." In compensation, they seek the vicarious thrill of watching others compete or live dangerously.

I do not mean to suggest that you must be a hunter or athlete to succeed in the investment world. What I do say is that both successful hunting and investing entail similar mental attitudes. Both involve taking risks in the hope of gain, but the risks that you must learn to take are not physical but entirely mental. There are very good reasons why the hunter and speculator think alike: both face the same kind of problem. When the hunter goes out into the forest, he is never sure whether he will find his quarry. When a speculator puts his money down, he is never sure where the market will go. Both hunter and speculator, no matter how well prepared, face total uncertainty.

This is not the world that we usually deal with, the world in which we get up in the morning and go to work where the only imponderables are whether the car will start or whether a customer will be friendly or whether our lunch date will have to be changed. These uncertainties are such minor deviations that they don't worry anyone who isn't neurotic.

To become a successful hunter in the financial markets, the first thing you should do is to question your own motives. Do you really want to be a hunter? Do you simply want to make money or are there other reasons for your interest in investing? These are not facetious questions. You may want to play the market to have an adventure, to impress your friends with your daring, to show them how smart you are. There are many reasons why people invest and not all of them are what you would expect.

A few years ago, a $100 million investment swindle surfaced. It had to do with a firm in California that offered the opportunity to make enormous profits by investing in syndicated oil leases. The return to those who got into the deal early was indeed very high, but it turned out that the original investors' "profits" were monies taken in from those who came along later. None of the millions invested with the firm were actually put into oil speculation. It was the kind of pyramid fraud that comes along every decade or so.

The interesting thing about this particular swindle was that the people who were defrauded were mostly well-known business leaders: board chairmen, company presidents, bankers, insurance executives and publishers. The victims were dozens of the men who are quoted in the financial press every week, the kind of people who would not be expected to have fallen for such a scheme. Naturally, few of the big names were willing to discuss their embarrassing mistake. But, here and there, some of the story leaked out. One chairman told a friend of mine that he'd heard about the deal in the locker room of his club from another chief executive who, he assumed, had good information. The chairman went along and urged his friends to do likewise. Thus, the confidence game grew until over $100 million had been put into it.

The man who conceived this scheme must have been a superlative student of male psychology. Each of the affluent victims not only wanted to be in on a good thing, but he wanted to invest because a friend was investing and, in turn, he wanted other friends to join him in the deal. Many of the investors put up their money probably because they were afraid not to, fearful that the friend who told them of the opportunity would interpret any reluctance as a lack of trust and might think someone who did not want to invest was indecisive, frightened, or lacked daring. In the end, it turned out that not one of the three dozen or so top executives who lost money in this fraud had bothered to investigate the deal at all. They had been attracted to it by the same kind of psychology that would animate a hunting band upon hearing a story of big game nearby. But they failed to act like real hunters. They did not investigate the quarry.

Peer pressure and wanting to be part of the group is another common, but unwise, reason for investing. When all the people at a cocktail party are talking about the money they've made in a particularly obscure Canadian oil stock or Australian mining company, it's a fair bet that the investment is either a swindle or that it's much too late to buy. When all of your friends are telling stories about how much they've made in gold or the stock market or Florida real estate or English antiques, it's a fairly good sign that prices are near the top and that you ought to be selling instead of buying. The hallmark of every major bull market since the late twenties has been universal public involvement. Those who recall 1929 say that not only all their friends were in stocks, but also cabdrivers, doormen, bootblacks, messengers. It should have been a warning, just as the same phenomenon should have been a warning in the late sixties. Very widespread market involvement means that large numbers of unsophisticated people are speculating in things they know little about in the belief that a new era of endless prosperity has come. This is not a hunting attitude but a "something for nothing" attitude. Hunters know that hunting is almost always difficult or dangerous. When it's easy, it's simply good luck—and a hunter does not depend on good stories or good luck.

Sometimes people who have made their living in mundane ways are attracted to exotic or glamorous investments. A friend once called with the news that he had heard of some fabulous gold discoveries in the jungles of Brazil and he wondered if I would be interested in forming an investment group to go after the yellow metal. I pointed out to him that neither of us had any gold mining experience, we did not speak Portuguese and the Brazilian jungles were not hospitable to gringos. Also, we had no

41

idea whether, and under what conditions, the Brazilian government would allow foreigners to prospect for gold and make money at it. Just to get this information and take the steps to overcome the obstacles could have taken most of the funds my friend had to invest with no assurance of success.

I told my friend that his problem was that he had confused desire for adventure with desire to make money, a thing which many people do. If he wanted adventure, I suggested he put his money in Treasury bills and take a trip to Brazil on the interest. If he managed to come back alive, he would still have his money and some good stories to tell about his experiences. He had experienced the spirit of adventure common to hunting, but he could not relate it properly to a realistic action because the impulse was alien to his everyday life.

One way of finding out whether you are really interested in being a money hunter is to ask yourself whether you would truly be satisfied to be successful in the markets— and tell no one else but your tax accountant about it. If you can sincerely answer yes to this question, then your emotional attitude toward the hunt for profits is very good. Few highly successful traders ever gossip about what they do in the market or how much they have made or lost doing it. It is almost as rare for such men to brag as it is for a highly decorated soldier to describe the exploits behind his medals.

Much of the nonrational pressure to invest is tied in with ancient definitions of manliness, the normal desire of a man to prove to his fellows that he is as brave and tough as they are. Says Margaret Mead in *Male and Female*:

> the young male has a biologically given need to prove himself as a physical individual . . . in the past the hunt and warfare have provided the most common means of such validation.

In other words, you may find yourself buying stock to prove to your friends that you have the guts to take a chance. According to Lionel Tiger in *Men in Groups*:

> dares which young boys issue each other and their effort to achieve decisive drama in their play foreshadow the patterns of adult mastery which in part comprise the adult manly style.

These are impulses of the hunter-warrior, but undisciplined and not consciously directed as part of a way of life.

The average businessman sometimes knows less than his wife about investments—though he will rarely admit it because he thinks he *ought* to know about such things, or he thinks that his wife and their friends will think he *ought* to know. Just as every man is presumed to follow baseball and know about the machinery under the hood of his car, he's also expected to *know* about stocks and bonds. This feeling can not only drive a man to invest, but inhibit him from asking for good advice because he's afraid to seem unsophisticated to his stockbroker. For less macho men the opposite may be true. Investors who have spent a lifetime learning about a particular profession or industry will let a stockbroker talk them into making an investment in something they know nothing about. Some people take less time deciding how to invest the savings of a lifetime—sometimes in the millions—than they would in deciding on the purchase of a new car or a fur coat. Again, this is because they do not relate their trading or investment activity to the knowledge and attitudes necessary for successful hunting.

This is one reason why you are usually better off putting money into things you understand thoroughly even if other areas appear more profitable. A hunter would never hunt an animal whose habits he did not know. If you are a real estate developer, you should look at real estate stocks and REITs. If you are a lawyer, you might consider looking at companies with legal problems that are familiar to you. If you sell insurance, you might think about investing in that industry. One of the great pitfalls of trading and investing is that the grass often seems to look greener on the other side of the fence. By contrast, the hunting attitude is always realistic.

It was Guy Duroys, author of *Black Maxims*, who said, "you can have anything you want as long as you don't want it." While the aphorism is deliberately cynical, there is a subtle truth in it, particularly for the investor or trader. In most spheres of life, you have a better chance of getting what you want by going after it with determination, if not passion. A high degree of wanting is an essential ingredient in getting a Ph.D. or a law degree, completing a book, or going into business for yourself. The ability to work long hours and the capacity to overcome obstacles are important personality traits in this contest. A never-say-die attitude often assures the ultimate payoff. But hard work, or bureaucratic expertise, is not the way of the hunter-warrior. He saves himself for the big risks of life and the rest of the time, by contemporary standards, he would be considered lazy.

In trading or investing, the so-called work ethic does not apply. This is because when you commit your money to the purchase of stock, bond or commodity, you are betting on a future over which you have no control. Whether you have studied the situation superficially or extensively, your actual investment decision is not a commitment of time or energy but a commitment of judgment to action. No matter how much you may have studied the particular situation, probably there is more about it that you don't know than you do know. Therefore, it is possible that your judgment may be wrong. The tenacity that may have made you a tremendous success in the retail business could ruin you if applied to markets that are going against you.

There is an old stock market axiom which you may have heard before, "cut your losses and let your profits run." In other words, if you buy stock at $20 and it inexplicably goes to $18, your best move probably is to sell it instead of holding on and hoping to get out even, which is what most people do. By the same token, if you buy stock at $20 and it goes to $22, it is better to hold on than to sell out of fear of losing your profit. "No one ever went broke taking a profit," your broker may tell you but no one ever got rich taking small profits while continuing to hold on to losing situations. If the hunter finds the game is too difficult to take, he gives up or goes after easier game. His requirement is to eat, or in financial terms, to take home profits. There is no other purpose to the hunt.

Conditioned psychological behavior would be to hope that your $18 would go back to $20, and to fear that you may lose the profit of your $22 stock. In other words, you want someone else—the market in this case—to do something for you. Time and again, in hundreds of markets, successful market operators have found that, in order to be a success, a reversal of this psychology is required. He must hope for greater profits but fear growing losses. If a hunter is in a bad territory, he does not hope he will find game, he gets out. Learning how to cultivate this attitude carries us to a deeper level of psychology. The action of markets, more than most other areas of human activity, has the psychological characteristics of warfare. Buyers and sellers are in opposition like the armies on a battlefield; each individual investor or trader is alone. He must judge how the battle is going even as he participates in it. Thus the greatest premium is on clarity and objectivity. He should have as little emotional identification as possible with either the buyers or the sellers. In other words, psychologically speaking, he should not care. He should neither fear to lose nor be greedy for profits since either attitude may blind him to a clear understanding of the real situation. But more than not caring, he should be willing to lose, for only by being able to accept the worst possibility will he be free of fear. It is not always possible to win in a speculative situation, so risk must be accepted—or else don't go hunting. As one of the richest men in the world, J. Paul Getty once advised: "If you want to make money seek tension." Oddly enough, this is almost an exact description of the stance of the samurai warrior and of warriors in most societies since time immemorial.

For example, in the *Hagakure*, Jocho Yamamoto (1659–1719) on the way of the samurai declares, "While we live, death is irrelevant, when we are dead, we do not exist. There is no reason to fear death." By the same token, there is no reason to fear financial loss, particularly during unstable times. Either you have money or you do not and your sole concentration should be on the decisions that you make to protect it or make it grow. As Yamamoto explains the situation within the warrior frame of reference:

> In the last analysis the only thing that matters is the resolution of the moment. A samurai makes one resolution after another, until they add up to his whole life. Once he realizes this, he need never feel impatient, he need seek nothing beyond the moment. He merely lives his life concentrating on his resolution. However, people tend to forget this, and to imagine that something else of importance exists. Very few realize the truth. Learning to follow one's resolution without error cannot be accomplished before the passage of many years. But after one has reached that stage of enlightenment, even if one does not consciously think about it, one's resolution will never change. If one perfects a single resolution, one will be seldom confused. This is loyalty to one's belief.

How often have you heard people tell you they could have made a lot of money but they were afraid to take a chance? It is a truism of both trading and investing—the greater the risks, the greater the rewards. However, most people are always looking for a "sure thing." Or some kind of guarantee that their investment judgment will be correct. Others use financial markets to expiate guilt feelings and often lose money that they have made with great struggle and effort in their regular line of work. Few people consciously face the possibility of loss when placing their bets. Therefore, they lose the flexibility and coolness of mind that was the outstanding trait of the samurai warrior. For instance, the ancient samurai credo declares:

> I have no laws; I make self-protection my laws.
> I have no strategy; I make "free to kill and free to restore life" my strategy.
> I have no designs; I make "taking opportunity by the forelock" my design.
> I have no enemy; I make incautiousness my enemy.

In a confused economy and in dangerous financial markets, with no certainty that statements by public officials are true or that investment recommendations by anyone will always be sound, to be ready for action and open-minded, alert but relaxed, is the best attitude. In other words, it is necessary to have the attitude of the samurai warrior.

III

RULES OF THE MONEY HUNT

In all big game hunting, there is no substitute for really knowing the habits of your game and also the particular section you are hunting.

Elmer Keith
Guns and Ammo for Hunting Big Game

Hunting is not easy.

As we have seen, during the 15th and 16th centuries it was the sport of kings, and it is an arduous sport. Neither is investing easy. If it were, there would be many more stock-market millionaires around than there are. You can't be a successful hunter or an investor half-heartedly and without practice. If you want to make money in a market, watch it all the time—and hunt! A man who goes hunting once a year rarely comes home with game. Shooting at targets or clay pigeons is not the same as hunting because you really have not taken a chance in the woods and fields. For the same reason, making imaginary trades in stocks or commodity futures and checking your results in the newspaper—"paper trading"—is very different from putting your own money on the line. No amount of target practice will make you a hunter and years of paper trading will not make you a successful investor. However, if you are an experienced hunter, you must also learn how to wait. You can't make a killing every day.

The following maxims were written early in the century by Horace Kephart, a famous woodsman and hunter of the time. They are as true today as when he wrote them and many of the admonitions relate not only to the hunt for animals but to the search for profit in the investment jungle.

▶ 1. *Hunt one kind of animal at a time and think about it.* A hunter who is going after ducks, but carries rifle slugs for his shotgun in case he comes across a deer, and has a .22 pistol on his hip for rabbit, is not likely to come home with anything. In the investment world it is better to put all your eggs in one well-chosen basket than to scatter them in many different investments and markets. There's no way you can intelligently follow a long list of investments unless you have no other occupation. Moreover, a number of investments tends to act like a small mutual fund: the winners are evened out by losers and your overall performance is not likely to be very good. Most highly successful traders and investors have concentrated on one thing at a time, whether it be cotton futures or gold or semiconductor stocks or old photographs. They take the time to learn about what they're investing in and they think about that investment constantly. Know whether you are after the gazelle of short-term profits or the elephant of capital gains.

▶ 2. *Know its [the animal] strong points and its weak ones.* In hunting, the advice is obvious. You need to know the habits of the animal, where it feeds and where it sleeps and when and how it is likely to move. In the markets you need to study your trading and investment possibilities carefully. Do not trust to luck. Try to understand the forces at work that tend to affect the price of your investment.

As another of the world's great hunting experts, Elmer Keith, expressed it:

> In all big game hunting, there is no substitute for really knowing the habits of your game and also the particular

section you are hunting. Experience learned in any one country will always help you in a new country, but a guide who really knows that particular section and the feeding and bed grounds of the game will be of inestimable value, regardless of how long you may have hunted. One man can hunt alone to better advantage than with a companion, unless he and the companion have hunted together for a time and each well understands the other's movements. But never should more than two men hunt together. Three is always a crowd and too noisy.

This of course would not apply if you were hunting big game with primitive spears. Then, you would need greater numbers, but more organization and discipline.

▶ 3. *Know where to hunt and where not to.* A hunter avoids the places where his quarry is not likely to be. In the marketplace it means that you should pay little attention to what your friends are doing or what the financial press is excited about. In general, hunt where you hunt alone; avoid crowd psychology. Don't fight the trend by sticking with a bad investment. When one market is doing badly another one may be doing well.

▶ 4. *Choose favorable ground.* For the hunter this means selecting a position that enables you to see the game before it sees you. In investing it means that, all other things being equal, you should be involved in the kind of investment where you stand the greatest chance of making the most money. The same amount that you may have to put up for an antique French armoire may give you control of 12 million yen in the currency futures market. On the other hand, don't overreach yourself. It is better to hunt rabbits and bring a few home, than to hunt bigger game and return empty-handed. Know your limitations as a hunter: discover the kind of game you are good at hunting.

▶ 5. *Consider the animal's daily habits.* In the forest, it's obviously necessary to know when the animal feeds and when it rests. In every investment market, there are patterns that can be identified. For instance, on an average day, the stock market typically opens flat and rises slightly for an hour or so. Weakness sets in around noon as the brokers go out to lunch. There's a rally around 2:00 P.M. when they return, then prices drift lower until the close, when there can be another rally. This doesn't happen every day, but it happens often enough to make a predictable pattern. Another example: the impact of the rate of inflation on the price of gold is like the footprints of the animal. Rising inflation always leads to an increase in the price of gold. War and rumors of war, as traders know, usually make the gold price leap.

▶ 6. *Know just what to look for.* The skilled hunter knows his target well enough so that he can track it through the woods by following footprints in the snow or soft earth, and by seeing signs of eating and droppings. An experienced trader also gets to know the signs and portents of the stock ticker and the charts of commodity trades.

To quote Keith again:

Game eyes are trained: you are not born with them. It is only natural that the man raised in the hills, who has been hunting livestock and game from earliest childhood and also practicing the trailing of game, should be the more adept. Still the novice can learn in time and can soon improve his game eyes with a little intelligent study and use. Spotting game in Africa is not so different from spotting game in North America. One of the hardest animals of all to spot, believe it or not, is the largest. Put an elephant in thick cover and you walk right up to him without seeing him, unless your eyes are trained. I didn't have the trouble most Americans do in going over there, but it's surprising how well the gray ghosts blend into the trees. Their legs look more like tree trunks and the patches of shade and sunlight that hit their bodies camouflage them to an extent that is unbelievable.

Many people believe that finding trading and investment targets is extremely difficult, but often the opposite is exactly the case. Like an elephant in the bush, some of the most potentially profitable opportunities are right in front of you, although other people may not be able to see them. For example, it was clear in 1974 that double-digit inflation had not been permanently defeated and long-term bonds of all kinds would become disastrous investments. This conclusion was supported by all the economic and financial history since the dawn of industrial civilization. Yet even those who anticipated continued inflation were reluctant to sell bonds short, and there was in fact a time-lag before long-term bonds collapsed, since the average buyer wasn't aware he was on the edge of a bear market as big as an elephant.

Another example was when gold went above $800 an ounce in early 1980 and silver reached $50 an ounce. It was as obvious as an elephant that these metals had far outrun the prices of other commodities and even the wildest projections for the rate of inflation. Yet nobody was talking about shorting gold, rather there were predictions in the newspapers that gold would go as high as $5,000 to $10,000 an ounce. It takes nerve and strong financial reserves to short a soaring market and such a move would be extremely unwise for the ordinary investor but every trader and investor can remember that no tree grows to the sky. As it was, in early 1980, the only individual we know who made a killing on the short side of gold was Dr. Armand Hammer, founder of Occidental Petroleum, who had already made several fortunes in oil and manufacturing. All his life, Dr. Hammer has been a natural money hunter.

► 7. *Maneuver according to a definite plan.* The hunter, even though he's aware of uncertainty, always has a plan in mind as he stalks his game. You should have the same attitude toward investments. If the price of your stock or financial futures contract is rising, you should have some definite notion of when you would consider selling or, at least, what kind of market action would prompt you to sell.

► 8. *Work against the wind, or across it.* Obviously, the hunter is aware that most animals have a sharp sense of smell and they try not to let the wind give them away. In my experience, big traders are secretive about their position, always using several brokers or banks to escape market detection. For the average investor, the message is: Don't let the brokerage house commission hustler or tipster pick up your scent, then you can't be influenced. Be something of a contrary thinker and keep your own counsel.

▶ 9. *Move noiselessly and reconnoiter carefully.* The hunter does not go stomping through the woods with equipment rattling if he's hoping seriously for a kill. Again, I suggest that there's an analogy in investing: If you are a large investor, don't give yourself away by ostentatious calls to brokers for quotes or information before you buy or sell. Don't look for reactions from others to your decision or ask for reassurance. Be resolute; accept responsibility for your decisions.

▶ 10. *Try to see the game before it sees you.* The careful hunter tries to get as close to the animal as possible before revealing himself. In the world of investments, you might think of this advice in terms of trying to be as sure as possible before you act. But when you act, don't wait for certain confirmation; act quickly. As a Lebanese trader once said, "opportunity passes like a cloud." One example: after several disastrous plane crashes a couple of years ago, the Federal Aviation Administration withdrew flight approval for the McDonnell Douglas DC-10 and the company's stock plunged in a few days. As the investigation of the airplanes began, some investors decided that the chances were very good that the plane would be recertified. After all, they reasoned, the DC-10 had flown millions of passenger miles safely so it was unlikely a design flaw was the cause of the crashes. The logical investment decision was to take a large position in McDonnell Douglas options. In the following month, those who did so made a 300 percent profit on their investment just as newspaper stories began to appear that the plane was going to be declared safe. By the time the official announcement was made it was, of course, too late to make a profit.

▶ 11. *Keep cool.* Sometimes this is the hardest advice for a hunter or investor to follow. But those who lose their heads are likely to lose a lot more. Always remember, your health, and in the end, your life is more important than money. However, keeping cool in the investment arena, as in game country, requires practice. It is better to take a series of small positions you can sleep with and learn the feeling of winning and losing before you "bet it all" and risk losing heavily. If you are uncomfortable with your investment, get comfortable and you will find clarity. No matter what you miss, there will always be another opportunity.

▶ 12. *Never fire at anything until you are absolutely certain it is not a human being.* Inexperienced soldiers firing "at anything that moves" often waste ammunition and kill their own people. Inexperienced investors, obsessed with fear and greed, often kill off their own chances for profit, or burn up their financial ammunition. In markets, this is often called overtrading.

▶ 13. *Never fire a shot that is not the best you can possibly do.* For a hunter, it will waste ammunition and cause the animal to flee. For an investor this means not making an investment decision that is not one you are satisfied with. Avoid the feeling that you simply have to invest. If you are not sure, don't.

▶ 14. *After firing, reload instantly.* A hunter must be prepared for the need of a second shot in case the animal may attack or get away wounded. In the marketplace, it means that you must always be ready to get out of the stock or commodities you have just purchased for another investment decision, perhaps the reverse of the one you have just made, possibly a decision to stay liquid until another target presents itself.

▶ 15. *If you wound an animal, don't follow immediately on its track, unless you are sure it is shot through the heart.* Many a hunter has been hurt or killed by wounded game. In financial terms, if your initial investment decision doesn't look like a winner, don't add to your position, recklessly pushing deeper into an uncertain situation. But there is a hunting tradition that you must not leave wounded game: finish it off. In markets, the corollary would be: don't let potential profit turn into a loss.

▶ 16. *Be patient over ill luck, and keep on trying.* Patience in the marketplace is essential. If you have missed an opportunity don't chase the market. Let it go and turn your mind to other possibilities. As a hunter does not have to hunt every day, you don't have to trade every day. Don't waste ammunition, arrows or dollars. The important thing is to have the ammunition when the real opportunity appears.

Finally, and somewhat simplistically, it is worth remembering that in order to hunt game you have to go into the woods. In other words, you have to be where the action is and be prepared to take risks. As I said before, if you want to make

59

money in a market, you must be in the market—not just thinking about it.

Another vital requirement for success is that, like a hunter in the bush, you must be able to make a decision without depending on the opinions of others. Miyamoto Musashi, the samurai sword-saint, called this "crossing at a ford." In the words of Musashi:

> "Crossing at a ford" means, for example, crossing the sea at a strait, or crossing over a hundred miles of broad sea at a crossing place. I believe this "crossing at a ford" occurs often in a man's lifetime. It means setting sail even though your friends stay in harbor, knowing the route, knowing the soundness of your ship and the favor of the day . . . . To cross at a ford means to attack the enemy's weak point and to put yourself in an advantageous position.

Speed of decision is also part of the samurai tradition. To quote Jocho Yamamoto: "Make up your mind within the space of seven breaths." When one proceeds in a leisurely fashion, seven out of ten actions turn out wrong. It is extremely hard to make decisions when one is flustered. But if, without worrying over minor issues, one approaches the problem with a razor-sharp mind, one will always reach a decision within the space of seven breaths.

Now we come to the question of how you can learn to have the qualities of patience, concentration and fearlessness that will make you into a successful financial hunter. If you have the desire and will to be a hunter and you are not going to enter the marketplace just because everyone else is doing it, you can mold yourself into a hunter who will be virtually guaranteed success. Anyone can do it who really wants to do it. Hunting for profits does not require the strength and stamina needed for an African safari. Investors are not born, they learn their craft and, inevitably, make some very expensive mistakes.

One of the first attitudes to get over is the feeling of helplessness in the face of massive and mysterious economic forces, the feeling that you are in the grip of events over which you have no control, the fear that somehow the game of life has been rigged and that you will never be able to win on your own. This sense of powerlessness is the myth of mass man. The justification for big government is the thesis that man basically is incapable of looking out for himself. It is an insidious and demoralizing idea that has been fostered for years by the elite government establishment and encouraged by most social legislation. The hunter, on the other hand, knows that he faces the powerful forces of nature—heat, cold, storms—but he also has the plans and means to cope with them and the confidence that he can survive. He accepts the mystery of natural forces with an almost religious awe.

If you are happy to have "Big Brother" assume the responsibility for many of the decisions in your life, you are not likely to want to become a hunter in the first place. But too many people think they have no choice. The division of labor in the family and society and the technological interdependence of our civilization makes us all feel less independent, less able to take care of ourselves in an emergency. Yet we sell ourselves short in holding such beliefs. In an emergency, when people are thrown on their own resources, they often find a surprising joy in their newfound ability to cope. During a recent transit strike in New York City, for example, millions of people suddenly found themselves walking to work. There was some real hardship, but many people found walking or bicycling more pleasant than waiting in line for a crowded bus, and some kept walking long after the strike was over. This is a relatively mild example of what happens to people during revolution or war. Senseless or not, war and violence are as natural a part of man's heritage as are his opposite urges for peace and comfort.

Above all you must overcome the idea that you have no power. You are not really at the mercy of your boss, your business or the environment. What you think is what you are. The outside world can reach you only through the mind. When forced by circumstances, most people find that they can do much more than they thought they could. After all, you are descended from hundreds of thousands of generations of hunter-warrior ancestors who survived challenges that we can imagine only dimly. You have the capacity to think for yourself and there are a thousand ways for you to form habits of independence.

While I deplore the survivalist philosophy of stocking a cave with dried food and buying a gun, there is a psychological point to it. You may never use the gun, but if it gives you a feeling of confidence, it has served a valuable purpose. Other activities can work equally well. Learn a trade or craft other than the one at which you make a living. Study another language. Take up one of the martial arts. Go on a long cross-country hike with minimal equipment. Start to jog.

The jogging boom may have crested in America, but it's still the most popular sport in the land. In terms of the gloomy feelings about our national future, there may be an unconscious element at work in fostering the widespread interest in jogging. Some long-buried Jungian memory may be prompting us to get ready for a tougher future. Animals grow their thicker winter fur long before the cold weather arrives. Could man somehow be acting out a similar instinct by jogging, of which the least may be the health value of the exercise itself? It gives the individual a chance to meditate away from the interruption of the telephone and the quote machine. Bodily activity calms and at the same time stimulates the mind. The beauty of the park in which I run is pleasurable. Beyond that, jogging is the only sport in which a relative beginner can engage and feel that he can compete with the best. I can choose to enter a marathon and, though my chance of winning may be remote, I can run against the best in the world. You do not have that choice in tennis or golf or swimming, but jogging does offer it and that is another reason for its popularity. People who, in their entire lives have never been athletically inclined, can buy a pair of running shoes and go out and discover that they can run farther and faster than they ever thought possible. If you have not tried jogging, I urge that you do so. In effect, physically learn to move easily as, in fact, the hunter-warrior always has learned to do.

In the investment world you have the opportunity to compete on equal terms with the professionals. You can outhunt anyone. When you buy shares on the New York Stock Exchange or gold futures on the Commodity Exchange, you have entered the same arena occupied by the shrewdest and best investors in the world. The remarkable thing is that you have certain advantages. The professionals have computers and multimillion dollar research budgets, but, in recent years, the biggest of them also have had miserable records at managing money. You can learn to match wits with them and beat them at their own game because they are slower to react, they tend to move in the same direction and, because of the institutionalization of this kind of investment, they take very few risks on their own.

For the reasons I have explained, the hunter attitude is akin to that of the samurai warrior and this, in turn, is closely related to the attitudes of mind and body developed by a study of Zen, yoga, transcendental meditation and the martial arts. A study of Eastern philosophies shows a direct correlation between the meditative state and the warrior's frame of mind. The cultivation of these attitudes for your personal and financial survival and prosperity lies in studies of one or more of these traditions. I will not attempt to describe fully any of these techniques, for there are books and courses available on all of them and many other related disciplines. However, all have certain things in common:

- *Discipline.* You should take up an activity such as swimming or jogging that you do every day for the sake of disciplining your body and mind.
- *Meditation.* You need a quiet place, a time to contemplate and reflect. It doesn't literally have to be a quiet room, though meditation is easier in such a place until you learn to do it no matter where you are.
- *Clarity.* You need to be able to quiet your mind, to stop the buzzing, booming confusion of thoughts that race through it much of the time.
- *Positive thoughts.* Samurai advice is never even to joke about making a mistake or being a coward. This sets up unconscious negative thinking.
- *Love.* Your life must include some part that you give to others. Remember, the hunter, by tradition, is a sharer.

Beyond these things there is the development of the right "battle attitude" for investing. Hunter-warrior traditions all maintain that most confrontations are not won or lost physically, but in the mind. But you cannot assume you will develop hunter-warrior attitudes automatically, or from reading this book. They must be practiced continuously, and in specific ways.

To condition your mind for what could be dangerous action, you should make a practice of remembering occasions when you were extremely successful and replaying them in your mind. Look for an image of power that you associate with it and call it to mind. For example, you might have been a successful high school football player. Call that to mind. Or you might have actually been a successful soldier, a real warrior. When faced with a work or financial situation, use your imagination to relive those occasions in war when you functioned most successfully. Many former soldiers who have trouble readjusting to civilian life don't realize that our economy is only a different kind of battleground with different rules, and the same attitudes transposed from war to the marketplace can work for you in a similar way.

Another aid can be consciousness raising, as it is taught through est, and various movements derived from Buddhism and other Eastern religions. Strangely enough, these teachings are designed to free you from the bondage of material things, social patterns of thought, and human passions, including a passion for money. But, equally strange are the facts that the objectivity of these attitudes is exactly what you need to make money, and that they spring from the same source as samurai fighting traditions.

If you want to get a concrete idea of what a truly objective attitude may be, think of its reverse, which would be investing money for your relatives. If you ever have done this, you know you soon become trapped in all the conflicts and mandates of family life, which are always nonobjective and emotional.

There are, in spite of all our training, things that will get in the way of peak performance in the investment world. The most insidious of these is fear: fear of commitment, fear of failure and, oddly enough, fear of success. One of the best ways to overcome fear is to act as if you are not afraid (even though you feel that you are) and your fear will often disappear. Another, of course, is to face your fear. If you are afraid of losing money, make a bet and lose some. See how it feels when the world does not come to an end.

Fear of success is a fear you may not be aware of, but if you have it, you must find it and defeat it in order to become a successful financial hunter-warrior. Psychiatrists since Freud have noted this as a problem and offered various explanations, many of them focusing on the feelings of guilt in some people that success seems to produce. The fear grows from an association of money with social status. You may feel that you did not deserve to be rich. Often this comes from family conditioning. You may have been conditioned by your parents to believe that getting rich is something other people do, or that "money is the root of all evil." That is why, when dealing with investments you should be sure, at the same time, to have a part of your life reserved for the process of giving love—or even money—to others.

Sometimes, money itself, especially in large amounts, often seems to affect people in strange ways. It is not for nothing that it has been called a god: Mammon. Men have long strived for it, worshipped it and feared it. It is far beyond being merely a medium of exchange or a store of value. Ernest Becker, Pulitzer prize-winning author of *The Denial of Death,* thinks that modern civilization has erected Mammon as a symbol of immortality—that there is a belief that through the possession of monetary wealth and many possessions, the individual could transcend time and space and achieve a kind of earthly immortality. This is because quite literally wealth does represent power. Money is equated with power of movement, power over people, even the power to transcend one's past and reach a new plane of material existence. Money is thus both attractive and frightening. To the hunter-warrior, however, money is only "bread," the means for survival, and he takes only what he needs. Therefore he does not have to be emotionally confused or overwhelmed by the money hunt.

In modern culture, money relates to the basic idea of mastery over nature or our environment. The concepts of the planned society and the controlled economy are part of the application of the so-called scientific method to the problems of our society. In this context, money, previously merely a commodity or a receipt for a commodity, becomes the measure of all things. As Norman O. Brown says in *Life Against Death: The Psychoanalytical Meaning of History:* "money reflects and promotes a style of thinking which is abstract, impersonal, objective, quantitative, that is to say the style of thinking of modern science and what can be more rational than that?" On the other hand, Brown points to the fact that the "instinct of psychoanalysis—which it represses—makes it want to attack the rationality of prudential calculation and quantitative science . . . ." Recent discoveries in quantum physics reveal that the world is not really as "scientific" as we had thought. There is even an "uncertainty" principle in modern physics that the hunter-warrior could have easily understood.

There is not space here for a lengthy discussion of Brown's famous essay, "Filthy Lucre." However, he makes it clear that much of the alienation and unhappiness of modern man has its origins in his money complex. By abandoning the religious, the mystical and the spiritual aspects of life, the mechanistic society provides no escape from selfishness (self-interest) or, more traditionally, the doctrine of Original Sin. "The illusion that Christ redeemed is abandoned," says Brown, "but not the illusion that Adam fell, and therefore, man must punish himself with work. The economy unconsciously obeys the logic of guilt." Without a sense of oneness with his universe and a feeling for the mystery of life, which the hunter often feels deep in the trackless forest, modern man finds himself in what Max Weber has called the "iron cage" of a mechanistic materialism. He is no longer part of the world.

Thus, in a strange McLuhanesque kind of way, money—the animal of our quest—becomes one of the obstacles of the hunt. This is because today money is hunted for its own sake—the sense of purpose of the hunt has been lost. Often, instead of being directly related to survival, it has become only sport, or "keeping up with the Joneses." Interestingly enough, however, money is not an animal; it has no feelings. Therefore there is no need to identify with it as has the historic hunter with animals. When relieved of its symbolism, money is only a means to other ends. It has, in itself, no humanity. Therefore, it can be hunted with the deadly calm of the most deadly samurai warrior.

IV

HUNTER VS. COMPUTER

Travel can be conducted safely in the jungle if you do not panic. If alone in the jungle, depending on the circumstances, the first move is to relax and think the problem out. . . . There is a technique for moving through jungle; blundering only leads to bruises and scratches. Turn the shoulders, shift the hips, bend the body, and shorten or lengthen, slow or quicken your pace as required.

"Survival, Evasion and Escape"
U.S. Army Field Manual 21-76

A HUNTER CANNOT BE successful until he comes to terms with his environment and has learned to walk through forest or jungle silently and easily. The first time a neophyte plunges alone into the woods he usually panics. Strange insects buzz around his head, branches slap at his face and arms, thorns tear at his flesh; he tries to protect himself and he slips on moss or trips over a root and falls. A genuine feeling of terror can envelop someone who finds himself in a jungle for the first time. Every vine looks like a snake, the screeches of strange birds seem like wild animal calls, the insects may be poisonous. If you are alone, the shock of the unknown may easily be compounded by getting lost. Suddenly, all the trees look alike and you are shaken by the realization that you don't know where you are or which way to go.

A veteran woodsman once described the feeling this way:

> Instantly, the unfortunate man is overwhelmed by a sense of utter isolation, as though leagues and leagues of savage forest surrounded him on all sides, through which he must wander aimlessly, hopelessly, until he drops from exhaustion and starvation. . . . He starts to retrace his steps, but no sign of footprint can he detect. He is seized with panic and fear. . . . It will take a mighty effort of will to rein himself in and check a headlong stampede. . . . In such a predicament as this, a man is really in serious peril. The danger is not from the wilderness, which pitiless niggard though it be to the weak-minded or disabled, can yet be forced to yield food and shelter to him who is able-bodied and who keeps his wits about him. No: the man's danger is from himself.

71

In many ways, the same sort of threatening environment will face you in the financial market jungle. The terrain is strange and unstable, the natives speak an odd dialect of English that's difficult to understand and which they dislike translating for visitors. They watch TV sets that display complicated charts and graphs, they scan flickering electric signs of moving numbers. The telephone is glued to their hand. There is muted noise and the feeling of intense time pressure. It is almost like being lost in a Middle Eastern bazaar, unable to speak the language, and keenly aware that the local thieves would probably cut your throat for the contents of your wallet. It is not a good atmosphere in which to make a bargain.

You are at a terrible disadvantage in the financial market jungle. The natives are out to sell you something and, though they may know no more than you about the future course of the market or the economy, they will tell you that they do and press you to make an investment before it is too late. But if you are lost in the investment woods, you must realize the worst thing to do is panic or let yourself be panicked into doing anything before you've had a chance to sit down and think about it. Don't throw your money at an investment the way some people feed coins into a casino slot machine.

You need to practice to be able to deal successfully with the market jungle, and the only way to get practice at investing is to put up some money and make a bet. No matter how small your investment, an actual bet will teach you more about the financial markets than all the books about how to make money by investing. You cannot become a hunter by reading about it: you have to go into the jungle and hunt. If you let a broker make your investment decision for you, he's getting some practice but you're not.

I will not offer specific advice on what stocks to invest in or what commodities to buy and sell. No hunter will give you precise rules for tracking down any particular kind of game because every day and place is different. All you need to know is how to hunt. Hunters never know ahead of time whether they will find what they're looking for or if, when they find it, they will make a kill. Theodore Roosevelt, a big game hunter, wrote in 1908, "On my hunting trips I have often had to hunt a long time before getting into good game country, and have sometimes made complete failures of hunts through not getting where there was any game at all."

My purpose is to teach you how the investment jungle works and where the game is likely to be at different seasons. I do not pretend that the hunt for profits is easy. Quite the contrary. You should not invest or speculate frivolously; it is a serious business. Neat systems for "beating" the market and formulas for getting rich are almost always fraudulent. A popular book of the 1960s described how an untutored investor had made millions in the stock market with his own unique charting system. If the man had indeed made as much as he claimed without paying taxes (which could have been true, as I recall, since he was not an American citizen and he operated on very low margins available to him in certain foreign countries), he did so with a chart system that was neither new nor original. I cannot guarantee that my advice will make you rich, but I do say that the attitudes I advocate will protect you from the worst of what may lie ahead and, with some luck, may also help you make a lot of money.

Don't overhunt. Our primitive ancestors were very respectful of nature and did not approve of those who hunted far beyond their need for food. This ancient admonition can be taken in several ways: don't be too greedy and don't over-trade. There is an old saying on Wall Street that a bull can make money and a bear can make money, but a pig loses money. Jesse Livermore, the best known speculator in the first quarter of this century, advised that no one should trade every day, week or month. "There are only a few times a year," said Livermore, "possibly four or five, when you should allow yourself to make any commitment at all. In the interim, you are letting the market shape itself for the next big movement."

Don't follow the pack. When most brokers, investment advisory services and financial pages agree, they are often wrong. This is not invariably true, but it's true enough to suggest that you question very carefully what seems so obvious to everyone else. The old stock market adage that "the public is always wrong," is not quite true. The public is usually right during the middle of a market trend and often wrong at the beginning and the end of a move. The public rarely anticipates a rise in prices until it's so well along that the newspapers and television have discovered it. At that point, the mass of the investment public begins buying and drives prices higher still. Then, when prices have risen to incredible levels and the professional traders are selling, the public remains in the market in the belief that prices will go higher still. In short, the "public is wrong" adage means that unsophisticated investors enter the market too late and stay invested too long.

A useful way to avoid groupthink is to periodically sit down and meditate on the possibility that anything widely believed may be wrong. If everyone is certain that China will shortly attack the Soviet Union, consider the possibility that the

Chinese won't attack. Or that the Russians will attack China instead. Or that China will attack India. Or that nothing will happen. This approach is called contrary thinking and it's a good way to avoid errors based on obvious conclusions. Most people shy away from an opportunity that's "too good"—the man who offers to sell ten $1 bills for $5—but they forget that some obvious opinions about economics, the markets, politics and world affairs are also "too good" to be true. Being a contrarian is not simply assuming that everyone else is always wrong, it's a way of thinking: you take prominent assertions about things that interest you and chew them over in your mind by considering opposites and alternatives. Quite often, what is widely believed is believed because *somebody* wants it believed. It is also true in markets that when everyone is bullish, it means that everyone who is interested in buying has already bought. There are only sellers left. This explains the paradox that it is only when things appear the most gloomy that the reversal comes; also, that extensive optimism invariably precedes a fall. When everybody is convinced everything is all right, the odds automatically favor something going wrong.

The ancient hunter had to think about his living in terms of the cycles of nature. Unable to impose his will on the world, he learned to live with night and day, summer and winter, heat and cold, the mating season of animals, the hibernating time. The giant cave bears that roamed Europe in the Stone Age were among the most dangerous game that ancient man had to contend with, and yet we know that hunters killed many thousands of them by understanding that the bear was most vulnerable when just aroused from his winter sleep. As the Bible observes:

> To everything there is a season, and a time to every purpose
> under heaven. A time to be born and a time to die. A time to
> plant and a time to pluck up that which is planted.
>
> [Ecclus. 3:1-2]

Farmers have always understood the cycles of nature. Like
the primitive hunter, they had no choice. Even today, with
pesticides and chemical fertilizers and mechanized equipment, the farmer is well aware that the fat harvest years may
well be followed by lean years. Those who do not live close to
the soil arrogantly try to toss nature aside. Able to conquer
her by artificially turning night into day, cold into warmth,
and telescoping space and time with jet travel, modern man
often forgets that he is a puny animal living on a spinning
globe in space. Man is humbled only when unforseen cata-
clysms occur. He forgets that nature does not really march to
his tune until the earth quakes under him or the wind blows
the roof off his house or he's engulfed by a flood. Man takes
the blessings of nature for granted until the cycles of weather
turn against him. He is surprised and angry when there's a
drought or too much rain or unusually cold weather and
crops are damaged. Man is angry as if it were somehow the
fault of his science for not having forseen or been able to
change such events—the fault of nature herself in capricious-
ly interfering with the plans of man.

To understand the financial forests, it is essential to realize
that they are dominated by forces over which you have no
control, forces both natural and manmade. Imagine that
you're about to go hunting in a jungle preserve covered by a
huge astrodome. All the animals are wild and the plant life is
natural, but the environment is manipulated by scientists.
The men who press the buttons and pull the levers can ar-
range for an artificial sun to shine when it is really night out-

side the dome. They can make it rain when the weather outside is clear. You can hunt successfully in this strange jungle only if you realize that the basic forces of nature cannot completely be controlled. The astrodome people have eliminated the cycles of the day and seasons, but the animals still respond for the most part to their own instinctive drummer. The jungle is more comfortable for you than the real one would be, but the hunting may be quite erratic—unless you know what the men in the control room think they are doing.

The market jungle is torn between the natural forces in the business cycle and the men who tinker with it in Washington. Their interference has changed the more or less predictable tidelike cycle of economic expansion and contraction into a whirlpool full of unexpected crosscurrents and changes in direction. The men in the control room constantly try to adjust things to a more placid steady state, but they have no window into the economic astrodome so they can't see the effect of what they're doing until it's too late. It's rather like trying to fly a plane blind using the instrument readings of the previous flight.

Still, the scientific mind refuses to admit that it cannot control natural cycles and it continues to try despite a nearly unbroken record of failure. Perhaps we have learned to map the world so well that we've stopped looking at the ground; we would rather read our instruments than look out the window. Farmers and hunters know better.

It slowly becomes clear to anyone who has studied or experienced the economic crises of the past decade that something is radically wrong with conventional economic thinking. Not only have the establishment economists been unable to forecast the future with econometric studies but their record has, in fact, been poorer than that which would have been achieved by flipping a coin. If the economists were tribal medicine men, on the basis of the job of being able to produce rain by uttering mystical chants, they long since would have been banished or beheaded. Yet despite their poor record, most of us still consult the newspapers every day, or sit spellbound at seminars to hear what economic experts are projecting. Their forecasts are always accompanied by vast arrays of statistics, or mathematical equations, which have an almost hypnotic fascination for business people and politicians alike.

To ask seriously why the economists are so often wrong is to raise questions that go to the fundamental dynamic of society itself, and the way we think about ourselves. Yet, it is not difficult to get a general idea of what is wrong. Imagine that you are on a highway driving from New York to Chicago. You probably have a road map. The map tells you where you must turn to get on the Pennsylvania Turnpike, but when you get to Harrisburg you can't find the sign indicating the connecting point. You go back over the map carefully and become convinced that you have followed the map's directions completely accurately, yet the turnpike is nowhere in sight. Somewhat irritated, you stop at a gas station to ask directions. The attendant gives you a completely different set of instructions to reach the turnpike. You tell him that his instructions are contradicted by your map. Finally, more out of frustration than belief, you follow the attendant's instructions and you soon find yourself on the turnpike. Yet you are still troubled because the map did not indicate the entrance point and you resolve to ask further questions at the next gas station.

In going through this relatively common experience, you have committed one of the classic errors of scientific thinking. You have assumed the description of the clearly drawn highway system on the map to be accurate when it is not. Subconsciously, you regarded the highway system you were transversing, and the system described on the map, as one and the same. But as you painfully discovered, the map was not an accurate portrayal of the territory. Alfred North Whitehead called this "the fallacy of misplaced concretion." He refers to the assumption that the scientific description of an event or an experiment, with numbers on a blackboard, is the same as the experiment itself. Whitehead propounded this concept in an attempt to explain in part why the scientific world that evolved from the thinking of Sir Isaac Newton did not jibe with the experimental discoveries of modern physics. However, the mistake of confusing the description of a thing with the thing itself had been identified 2,000 years earlier by the Greek philospher Zeno, who postulated that the description of the flight of an arrow was not the actual flight of an arrow.

Modern economics uses numbers or mathematical equations to describe all economic events. Consequently, the economists think about these events in abstracts: numerical terms. Like the traveller, they look at the map instead of the territory and, in time, tend to believe that only the map is real.

Modern economic analysis evolved directly from Newtonian physics which held that time was an absolute, space was three-dimensional, and the elements which moved in this space were material objects or particles. Newton's famous law of gravity described the forces that govern the relationships between the objects, such as the sun and the earth. The universe was envisioned as a gigantic machine which had been put into operation by God. Newtonian mechanics was tremendously successful in explaining the movements of the planets and the basic features of the solar system. The scientific approach also led to a host of other discoveries and the development of numerous engineering techniques and the evolution of modern technology. However, in 1905, Albert Einstein, with the introduction of his special theory of relativity, started a revolution in the world of physics, which has completely changed man's scientific perception of himself and his universe.

Time was proven to be no longer an absolute, space was found to be curved, and, as far as the famous law of gravity was concerned, to quote the great mathematical theorist, Bertrand Russell who studied and explained relativity, "the sun exerts no force on the planets whatsoever."

The physical model for economic theory has been shattered, but most economists continue to use it anyway. Since economics is a practical, not a theoretical subject, using an incorrect theory is bound to produce mistaken conclusions. Over the short run, an economic theory, at least when it becomes popular, is just an abstract argument to justify the prevailing economic order. It is susceptible to being wrong at some point. Generally, the more theoretical an economic opinion, the more likely it is to be wrong. I call this the "no theory" theory of economics. In other words, the real economic world, contradictory, erratic and ever-changing, cannot be adequately explained by theory. It requires observation.

Economics is the key to understanding where the economy is going—the lay of the land, the weather and which animals should be hunted—and it is thus the key to decisions in the investment jungle. There are all kinds of forces and events that impinge on markets: weather effects, wheat prices and orange juice futures. Fear of war in the Middle East can affect the price of gold. Interest rates affect bond prices. But, the overriding force that affects every market is the cyclical movement of the economy. Is it in the early stages of a growth phase with plenty of capital investment opportunities available, or is it overextended with overbuilt plant, and shrinking credit? Before you put to sea, you must know whether the tide is going in or out.

There are many methods and theories of investment. Technical analysis, the literal study of price movement on charts, has a large following. Its adherents believe that the interpretation of the patterns traced by the daily movement of prices is the best method of forecasting the future of a market. Strict technicians are not interested in the real life fortunes of the company or commodity that lies behind the numbers. They believe, with some justification, that the only meaningful thing to consider is the action of the market itself. On the other side of the aisle, fundamental analysis concerns itself with the specific earnings and financial projections for individual companies and industries as a whole. Practitioners believe that the only way to divine the future of an investment is by studying the investment itself. Both methods can be useful and they are often used in tandem: if the fundamental analysis of a company is bullish and is confirmed by technical analysis, the outlook is considered more favorable than if the two approaches diverge.

Computers have become very important in market tactics. Programmed with historical price information and given instructions based on technical theory, they flash automatic "buy" and "sell" signals. Most of the money that moves in the stock market these days is responding to some kind of computer program. This is one of the reasons that the market has become much more volatile than it used to be. Technical analysts pretty much agree on the basic theory and if most of the computers are programmed the same way, they will all flash the same signal at the same time.

We still hear about the concepts of undervaluation and contrary opinion, but the job of managing the really big pools of investment money in our society today has been turned over to computers, which amounts to a very big cop-out. Even the military has tried to substitute increasingly more complex, electronically-directed weaponry for the individual fighting man. Science has fought nature and achieved some great successes, but at the cost of an atrophied natural instinct—the instinct for using and living with nature—the instinct of the hunter-warrior.

In a posthumous monograph, John von Neumann went even further saying unequivocally, "the language of the brain [is] not the language of mathematics." Quoting von Neumann, the mathematical economist Nicholas Georgescu-Roegen, in his little known work, *The Entropy Law and the Process of Economics,* says that "the reason no computer can imitate the human brain is that thought is a never-ending process of change." Yet there are nearly 150,000 economists in this country who are trained to use computers to make "econometric models" for investment and market decisions—models that Irving Kristol has called "a form of mathematical mimicry."

When the mathematical mumbo jumbo is torn away we are left with the computer-man's common lingo: "GIGO"—

"garbage in, garbage out"—meaning that the printout from the smartest and fastest computer in the world is only as good as the data fed into it. In other words, the computer can always extrapolate from the past, based on the data from previous economic experience, but it can never—as a human being can—deal innovatively with *changes as they take place.* Thus, in significant respects, an econometric projection is simply a vastly more complex form of technical market analysis. A stock that traces a "head and shoulders" chart formation is, according to the technician, supposed to decline. Similarly, when a computer-generated econometric model generates a certain pattern, the economy also is supposed to decline.

All this is not to say that computers have no value as projective tools. They are very useful in generating a picture of the future in terms of continuing trends; that is, what the economic situation will be assuming the present trend lines of the various components continue to move up or down at the same rate. Properly programmed, a computer is capable of almost instantly printing out an "economic future" based on a long list of assumptions. But, a crisis is essentially discontinuous—a sharp, unexpected break in the trend—and it does not really compute.

For example, though one postulate of economic decline is an increase in the total debt load, the prediction of precisely at what point this might produce a deflationary, or hyperinflationary, break would be arbitrary. Debt always exists in such a sea of other economic, political and social variables that the human intuition that encompasses all these factors is perhaps a better guide to the possibility and timing of collapse. When I refer to intuition, I don't mean second sight or precognition, though these phenomena may be possible. I am talking about the hunch or "gut feeling" that veteran traders seem to acquire after years of dealing with fluctuating markets. This is the meditative state of the hunter-warrior. The speculator Jesse Livermore often acted on what seemed to be hunches that were really his subconscious mind at work putting many disparate facts and bits of experience together until they formed a conclusion in the shape of an almost uncontrollable urge to buy or sell a stock. There is nothing really mysterious about this. Most of us have had the experience of waking from sleep with the answer to a problem in mind. The problem is that most people do not act on their intuitions—they wait for a message from the outside world, a political leader, or a computer.

For these reasons, as well as those stated elsewhere in this book, computers are an attempt on the part of money managers to "pass the buck" on investment decisions.

While traditional evaluation and contrarion beliefs have merit, in the day-to-day world of trading and investing, I believe a feel for market psychology is paramount. What is the behavior of the game and the attitude of the other hunters? Since the name of the game is money, your principal area of study should not be stocks or bonds or a particular commodities market, but money itself. Studies in economic history reveal that the most important single indicator of the future prosperity or progress of an economy and the rise or fall of stocks and bonds probably is financial liquidity—the supply of money relative to the transactional requirements for the exchange of goods and services, and the price paid for it, or interest rates.

In short, money makes the world go around. When money

is in short supply, the economic world moves slower; when there's a lot of money (by money we mean purchasing power), the economy speeds up. It's somewhat like the game "Monopoly": when most of the "money" in the game winds up in the hands of one of the players, the game is over. To start playing again, all the players have to have money and the more they are given, the faster the game goes and the longer the play lasts.

Yet, in the abstract, money is hard to define. Historically, money has been the subject of great theoretical debate focused on whether it is a commodity, or simply a medium of exchange, or a store of value; that is, whether money has intrinsic value. From one point of view, the money in your checking account—which is a deposit payable on demand— is not really money because it represents no tangible value, having value only in exchange for goods and services. Discussions of this sort are analogous to the medieval theological arguments over how many angels could dance on the head of a pin. What counts is what you will give and what you will accept as money.

Historically, no matter how it was defined or in what form it appeared, an increase in the supply of what was called money has been associated with prosperity since the dawn of organized society. Conversely, a scarcity of money has been associated with declines in economic activity. For example, the awakening of the world's commercial instincts after the Dark Ages was a direct result of the discovery of gold in the New World. Similarly, the great economic expansion of the first three-quarters of the 20th century was associated with the discovery by government that an increase in printing press money, unbacked by anything of tangible value, could have significant economic impact. This turned out to be true in spite of several earlier disastrous experiments with unbacked money.

When a currency has been depreciated, as the U.S. dollar has been in recent years, the relationship between the volume of money and economic activity becomes much more complex. The tracks in the market jungle become confusing and hard to follow. Money still makes the world go around, but price inflation tends to distort normal behavior. When money begins to lose value month after month for a year or two, businessmen and consumers change their money habits. People stop saving and investing and begin buying things with their money as soon as they get it. Businessmen go deeply into debt and use the money to buy assets; they know that the debt will be repaid with depreciated dollars and the value of the assets will rise as the value of money continues to fall. These are simple manifestations of inflationary psychology and, in the context of prolonged high inflation, they represent rational behavior. Any government that urges its citizens to buy savings bonds during a time of double-digit inflation is giving them bad advice.

Until inflation—the depreciation of money—gets out of control, the effect of the supply of money on economic activity can still be seen when the charts are recalculated in constant dollars, that is, dollars with the inflation rate taken out. In almost any modern period of inflation, the decline in real purchasing power of money has correlated rather well with the constant dollar value of common stocks.

There are a number of empirical correlations that can be derived from studying the history of the volume of money in relation to the amount of goods and services produced:

▶ *1. When the amount of money is increased while price inflation is near zero, interest rates dip at first in response to the "easy money" available. Then, after a lag of 18 months to two years, with very few exceptions, they begin rising as the larger amount of money stimulates business and creates a demand for still more money and ultimately, price inflation. Stock and bond markets usually rise under such conditions.*

▶ *2. As the rate of inflation increases, interest rates rise in tandem with it. Lenders want compensation for the declining value of the money they will get back, so they add the currently expected inflation rate to the traditional cost of money. Stock and bond markets fall as precious metals and gold stocks rise higher.*

▶ *3. When interest rates are raised sharply, the price of gold will fall, but only for a short time. Continued high rates signify inflation and correlate with a higher price for gold. By the same token, a sharp fall in the rates indicates a rise in the price of gold, but a continued decline in interest rates is recessionary which is negative for gold.*

▶ *4. The more rapidly the supply of money is increased, the faster it will lose its value. Consequently, the greater the need to create more credit or "print money" to make up for the lost value. This is the famous law of acceleration of issue and depreciation of Andrew Dickson White.*

In general, a reduction in the supply of money first produces a financial squeeze and then a recession or depression. With a lack of demand for money, interest rates will fall, inflation will decline and the price of gold will drop. Obviously, unexpected factors, such as an outbreak of war, can violently upset these cause-and-effect relationships. Moreover, money supply, interest rates, inflation and the price of gold are intertwined with many other measures of the economy which makes the relationship hard to follow. Washington adds to the difficulty by reporting statistics in a way that disguises what the people in the economic control room are really doing.

Still, the money supply, whether defined as M_1, M_2, M_3 or L, is the most reliable indicator of the economic future. Keep your eye on the money and pay only secondary attention to the rest of the statistical jungle. The hunt for money is big game hunting. Therefore, concentrate on the footprints of the elephant and ignore the rabbit tracks.

V

UNDERSTANDING THE FOREST AND THE TREES

Man's two great concerns since he has existed have been to create a network of traditions which he afterwards endeavors to destroy when their beneficial effects have worn themselves out.

Gustave Le Bon, *The Crowd*

A S GOETHE ONCE SAID, "coming events cast their shadows long." Therefore, a good money hunter should read the financial weather reports and study the position of the economic sun, which, since 1980, has been casting a long shadow indeed. Since the early 1970s, literally thousands of works have been published predicting runaway inflation, depression, economic and ecological breakdowns of all sorts, and social revolution. At one point, in fact, gloom and doom almost became a special segment of the publishing industry. A history of long wave economic cycles indicates this is another period in which a "great crash" will occur. Yet, as you read this, there is a high probability that the world you have lived in thus far in the latter portion of this century, will *not* have come to an end. You will have experienced economic depression, new high rates of inflation, chaotic securities and commodities markets, the breakdown or collapse of major portions of American industry, increased crime in the streets of major cities, and race riots. By now, you may have read about the collapse of a big multinational bank or group of banks and read about the introduction of foreign exchange controls, and probably wage and price controls. One school of thought holds that the economy will move into deflationary collapse. More likely, we could be in the midst of another feverish inflationary boom brought about by desperate credit creation and money

91

printing by the Federal Reserve. Whatever the situation, your attitude will be more important than any handy, formularized investment strategy you can read in a book.

The hunter had a medicine man to forecast the future; Greek warriors relied on the oracle at Delphi. However, unlike modern man's dependence on the scientific mumbo jumbo of the economists, the hunter-warrior depends on flexibility and adaptability to changing conditions. The idea of economics or even scientific certainty has been a relatively new development in the history of man. During most of his tenure on this planet, man has consciously lived with uncertainty. Not knowing whether it will rain, where the game is, or what tomorrow will bring is the natural condition of man; and, as our air-conditioned, statistics-happy, industrialized society stumbles and crumbles, it is time to reevaluate this vital part of man's psychological heritage.

When ready for battle, the samurai warrior does not engage in the exhaustive exercise of attempting to second-guess his opponent. Instead, he concentrates on "not knowing," on fixing all his attention on the eternal *now* from which all actions spring. He is ready to attack or defend in an instant, but his mind is empty. He is at one with what Musashi called "the void." Uncertainty is not his enemy: it is his way of life.

Modern Western man cannot hope to duplicate this trance-like state—at least not for long. We are creatures of a mechanistic society based on dogma of operations research and computerized projections. However, the individual can, through conscious effort, purge a great many fixed ideas from his mind, such as that there must always be "progress," that the government is obligated to solve his problems, or that it is wrong to sell a stock or commodity short. The hunter-warrior will go long or short as the occasion demands, or move quickly to new ground. He has very little interest in ideas—only survival and, of course, gain.

To believe in something—a political cause, a religion, a social form—can be very comforting and even heroic. However, it is the contention of this book that, *in uncertain times, the future often belongs to the man with the courage of no convictions.* The hunter, in contrast to the machine-age man, adapts himself to the seasons. He knows when to hunt deer, and when and where to go for small game. He follows the migrations of herds, and becomes a student of animal and seasonal cycles. He studies the long climatic shifts that can turn a savanna into a desert or a valley into a swamp. He knows that change is the first law of nature.

By the same token, the financial warrior scans the economic horizon and tries to appraise the several economic conditions and movements of popular mood and mass opinion. For instance, because of the politicians' love of the potential of unlimited power to appropriate money, and the citizens' demand for financial security at any inflationary cost— as well as the immense profitability of inflation to bankers and large corporations—there undoubtedly will be high inflation during the 1980s. At the same time, because we are a burned-out economy, we will see depression. It will be a period unlike that ever seen by American citizens before. It is a pattern known as "stop-go economics", which features alternating periods of inflation and deflation, like uncertain weather, like the days of late autumn before a bitter winter.

In the world of stop-go, there is, in reality, no economic sunset but a kind of perpetual twilight without final boom or bust. Instead, the Federal Reserve and the administration feed the populace uppers when the economy is experiencing a high, while the real economic fat of the country is burned off in the fires of inflation, and the vast pile-up of debts that are part of the process are liquidated through currency depreciation. The deflationary group of the doom-and-gloomers point constantly to the growing mountain of government and private debt. But currency depreciation makes debt fear a myth. For instance, at a 20 percent rate of inflation, an obligation to pay $100 billion a year is reduced by depreciation to $1.5 billion in real purchasing power over 20 years. It becomes a real obligation of only $50 billion in little more than three years.

Stop-go is no mystery to the finance ministers and economic pundits of Europe. England has been on the stop-go road for two decades (only very recently under the Prime Ministry of Margaret Thatcher have they made an effort to return to the economic straight and narrow). Stop-go has been more successful in France because, after more than 60 years of inflation, neither the French politicians nor the French people have any illusions about it. Consequently, like the contented occupants of a comfortable bordello, they have instituted policies and habits of life that make it work after a fashion. The best way for the individual to deal with stop-go is, again, to develop the "Attitude No-Attitude" of Miyamoto Musashi, the samurai *sensai* (teacher). Throw away your economics textbooks and *don't try to predict the future.* Simply learn to react quickly to government actions and reactions in the markets in which you have chosen to trade. As Musashi would express it:

> the primary thing when you take a sword in your hands is
> your intention to cut the enemy, whatever that means.

In other words, to make profits, preserve your financial life.

The central thesis of stop-go is that, once embedded in a society, inflation probably cannot really be rooted out. This, of course, is not true. There are a number of classic examples where inflation has been stopped dead in its tracks by the right policies, including the termination of the Great German Inflation in the 1920s. But permanent stoppage of inflation involves economic pain that no politician in office could survive. Therefore, they offer the public nostrums and hope. For, as everyone knows, whether you are an alcoholic or a spendthrift, it is easier to rationalize than to quit. Or, if you are a Frenchman you merely cut down the money printing a little from time to time. The control of the economy is maintained through credit allocation, foreign exchange controls, and the use of various other regulatory techniques, with credit controls as the keystone.

Perhaps the simplest explanation of stop-go that I have ever heard was over cocktails with Michel Rochard, leading financial genius of the French Socialist party and at some future time a possible president of France. At the time I spoke with him, the Socialists were trying to raise the minimum wage for Frenchmen by 30 percent—as a condition of their party taking power.

"How can the country pay for such an increase?"

"Print money," said Rochard.

"But that will cause roaring inflation," I said.

"Certainly," said Rochard.

"Well," I said, "what do you do about that?"

"Wage and price controls," said Rochard, "and credit controls."

"But then you'll have a recession," I said, "and the people

95

will be unhappy and your party may not be returned to power."

"Naturally," said Rochard.

"How do you solve it then?" I asked

"It's not a difficult problem," said the possible future President, "we simply offer to raise the minimum wage again."

Because of the one-and-a-half to two-year lag between the creation of money and its inflationary effects, stop-go economics is the politicians' dream policy. When the economy is sluggish and the rate of inflation is moderate, they stimulate it with massive monetary and fiscal injections. These have the immediate effect of stimulating business activity, raising employment and creating a relative degree of prosperity.

A couple of years later, when the increase in the money supply has produced a rise in the rate of inflation and people are getting upset, the central bank institutes a policy of monetary restraint. Political officials do a lot of talking about budget-cutting until the economy falters and a real economic contraction is not allowed to take place. Once things are sufficiently depressed for the National Bureau of Economic Research to declare that the economy is in recession and the fact is reported on the nightly television news, the government and central banks switch their policies from stop to all-systems-go. The staggering economy receives new monetary and fiscal injections and, like a junkie five days off heroin, goes into temporary euphoria. But the high is not as good as the previous one. Each injection of artificial financial liquidity has less effect than the last one. Consequently, the rate of price inflation due to currency depreciation ultimately ratchets up to higher levels, while the average citizen feels the squeeze with increasing degrees of intensity at his corner grocery store, and in his life style in general.

96

As many economic writers have pointed out, the inflation is actually a tax, since it depletes the citizen's purchasing power while increasing that of the government. However, there is a bright side. As total real purchasing power declines, at the same time, in almost miraculous fashion, the inflation is paying off the national debt as well as the debts of corporations, and your own mortgage and installment debts. As Sarah H. Miller, a perceptive business journalist, expressed it: "I still believe in inflation. I have to. I have lots of debts." And Sarah has lots of company.

For instance, conservatives continue to scream about U.S. government spending which was pushing well beyond the $600 billion a year level at the end of 1980. Yet, when allowances were made for the depreciation of currency, the budget, in terms of real purchasing power, or constant dollars, was not much higher than ten years ago. Interest on the debt for 1981 was estimated at $90 billion or a little less than $2 billion a week; however, in 1932 dollars, it would only be $9 billion. Arithmetically, currency depreciation behaves in the same way as compound interest except that the compounding is in reverse. For example, as I have pointed out, at a constant 20 percent rate of inflation, the government, or anyone for that matter, could go $100 billion in debt; after seven years, the debt would be $25 billion and after 20 years, it would amount to only $1.5 billion in real purchasing power—all without a single payment being made on the principal. But government records would still show it as a debt of $100 billion. If necessary, the process can be speeded up, so that the debt is virtually wiped out overnight through a combination of currency depreciation, debt repudiation, and authoritarian controls.

It is at this point, as many writers have warned, that a new currency could be introduced. For some odd reason, most otherwise intelligent world currency authorities, such as Franz Pick, imply that this is a terrifying event when in reality it is probably no worse than having your appendix taken out. France introduced a new currency in 1958 and, after a brief slump, it brought a brighter economic glow to the faces of 50 million Frenchmen. Even the worst inflation in modern history, the much written about Great German Inflation of the 1920s, was brought to a halt without an economic collapse through the introduction of the *rentemark,* which, despite a plethora of historical misinformation to the contrary, was not *backed* directly by gold or anything else of tangible value. Throughout history, new currencies for old have been introduced countless times after the old currencies have outlived their inflationary usefulness, and aside from the possibility of moral improprieties, the consequences have been at least temporarily beneficial. (Pragmatically speaking, it is just another technique in the arsenal of stop-go to insure that the members of the establishment remain established even though the inexperienced investor may lose his shirt.)

We expect stop-go to work better in the 1980s since its techniques depend on a government whose spending can influence the gross national product in an important way and whose bureaucracy is deeply entrenched and ready to regulate every aspect of your daily life.

For the individual investor, the problem of dealing with stop-go is not so much intellectual as it is emotional. It's like hunting in a swamp or over terrain with unstable footing or hunting in fog or rain.

In a very real sense, the stop-go society is very much like

the environment of the hunter: constantly changing, with different kinds of game—and opportunities—during different phases of the stop-go seasons.

But, while stop-go is more likely, it is not a certainty. A classic deflation at some point is possible, which will put an emphasis on cash and financial liquidity. It is also possible that Western civilization is moving toward the kind of collapse not seen since the fall of the Roman Empire, when the "lesser developed countries" of those days, the "barbarians," finally sacked and burned Rome, which had been virtually impregnable for 500 years. Our world money system is not based on reality, but on fiat money which is, in the end, a promise to pay for nothing. For the true hunter-warrior, such an environment could be paradise. For while others would be starving, he would be hunting among the ruins.

The image of the central banker as the stern financial father figure who will discipline the errant children of the marketplace has been with us almost since the inception of central banking in the 16th and 17th centuries. And, when the world was operating on a gold standard, it was a valid image since, under a commodity money standard, there was a point at which the financial cupboard would become bare. In the strange new stop-go world of the 1980s, however, while the central banker still waves his finger under the nose of commerce at the front door, he keeps right on passing money out the back door. He has the checkbook that is endless and he is willing to accommodate everybody. The only problem is that there is nothing real or tangible in his checking account—or in the whole banking system for that matter. It is a system constructed entirely on faith. It is somewhat like a religion: if you believe in it, it will help you. If you lose your belief, you lose all benefit.

Thus, it is not farfetched to imagine the great international banking system of the earth blowing away suddenly like leaves in a windstorm. The uncertainties of the early 1980s have already resulted in the little-noted fact that more than 25 percent of world trade is conducted on a barter basis. Money is losing its status. After a financial holocaust, each nation inevitably would draw closer within itself, and move away from money as the principal social mechanism toward a value system based on genuine productivity, a more tribal sense of community, and possibly a spiritual rebirth within the collective human psyche.

Barring global transformation, however, sooner or later, some new version of the money game will begin again, starting with sophisticated forms of barter. Meanwhile, hunter-warrior strategy would dictate that you aim for no fixed investment position or particular predetermined income level. Instead, you endeavor to ride with the tide of stop-go—buying go investments such as common stock during the go periods when money and credit are obviously expanding, and making stop investments such as gold and tangibles, when the money printing results in the inevitable currency devaluation. If in doubt, go for tangibles. But you must be alert for shifts in comparative price relationships. For instance, real estate, which was a marvelous inflation hedge during the 1970s, becomes less so during the early 1980s. This is because interest rates rose ever higher as terms of loans were constantly shortened. On the other hand, the home owner is probably the nation's most important voter and consequently will not be neglected by the politicians even under the worst of inflationary circumstances. What this means is special credit controls relating to mortgages and housing, further expansion of federal home loan programs, tax advantages, and so forth.

Big businessmen and speculators are able to profit from currency depreciation because they have large lines of credit and can count on paying back their loans in cheaper dollars. Government workers and members of powerful labor unions also benefit because they are covered by inflation escalation clauses. The poor do not do too badly since the government makes sure they have enough food stamps or whatever to keep them from trying to start a revolution. The only real sufferer is the retired individual living on a fixed income and the middle-class manager or professional person. The economy, of course, suffers because people become money mad instead of production-oriented, and the quality of products and public services continues to deteriorate. Ultimately, stop-go economics has to come to an end. The shift from a production-based society to a fiat-money society inevitably sets the stage for political and social revolution. These possibilities are enhanced by the fact that policy-directed inflation is introduced into most societies after a long period of economic expansion, such as we have witnessed in the United States, where the standard of living went up for a long time and the average individual gradually gained the impression that he would always be earning more and able to buy more in the years ahead. When the economy begins to top out and these private expections begin to be unfulfilled, then those in positions of authority, in an attempt to remain in power, introduce a false prosperity by using the inflationary printing presses. When the populace begins to see through this, the government introduces wage and price controls, credit controls, foreign exchange controls and whatever other regimentation is necessary. Thus, inflation is stopped for a while. Later the controls are taken off and the money printing presses are switched on again. As a last resort, as occurred in Germany in the 1920s and in France in 1958, a new currency is introduced which makes it possible to start the game all over again. In the end, stop-go is only a way of postponing the economic day of reckoning. However, you can grow old waiting for that day since, as the history of the U.K. and France have shown, stop-go can last for a long time. Meanwhile, if you learn the rhythms of stop-go and have some understanding of the economic and political forces at work, you can become a successful money hunter.

Once you understand stop-go, you will cease to be bothered by the proposition of quantum physics that there is no solid matter, only bundles of energy that seem solid, and will be able to accept this state with greater equanimity.

But there is one caveat that you should be aware of, and that is the peculiar psychological bent of some Americans to flee the country. Even during the most desperate inflationary days, most residents of Germany, France, Brazil and other countries never thought of leaving their native land for a safe haven "off shore," let alone moving all their assets overseas. The United States may be a monetary slaughterhouse, but it is the richest nation on earth in natural resources, food and a workforce educated in the use and direction of advanced technology. Only the Arabs have a compulsive desire to buy things in other places, and, if you ever cameled or motored across the deserts in the Middle East, it is not difficult to figure out why. Even with modern air-conditioning, the deserts of

Southern Saudi Arabia are not called the "empty quarter" by accident. If you ask the average rich Kuwaiti what he would do if his country were invaded, he would say that he would move to London or New York, where he is already keeping his money, his house, his possessions and perhaps even his mistress.

But let's look at a specific example of how you could make a killing in the stop-go world. Sometime during the 1983–86 period, the U.S. currency will be depreciated in order to facilitate payment of world dollar debts, public and private. One sign will be an accelerating pattern by lesser developed countries of defaults on loan payments to American banks. A sign of the looming crash of the dollar will be a deep decline in U.S. interest rates relative to those of other countries and a rise in U.S. inflation. To be in a position for a killing, you can short the dollar by buying Swiss francs, Japanese yen or German marks on the International Monetary Market in Chicago, so your funds never have to run the risk of possible block and seizure in other countries. But the currencies should be sold at the first whiff of foreign exchange control.

This is just one example of tactical thinking. The important thing to remember is that unstable and volatile markets, whether in currencies, stocks, bonds, or gold, are markets of opportunity—and your greatest assets are your talents and capabilities. Furthermore, if you want to make money (however defined), and get ahead in the world, move *into* the cities, not *out* of the cities, because that's where the greatest opportunities will be. Big cities are also a good place to be if you want to play a role in the great political changes that lie ahead. No revolutions were ever made in the country.

As we pointed out earlier, aside from its money confusion

and incapacity to run the world, the United States is poten-tially the most self-sufficient nation on earth with the greatest natural combination of mineral, energy and food resources. Time and again, history has proved that the collapse of a money banking system does not mark the end of a country. It may even be a prelude to economic rebirth.

As we've seen, the great ambition and conceit of modern man has been his control over nature. In some areas, the at-tempt to control has created a backlash. Seeding clouds to cause rain fell into disrepute when nearby counties and states complained that this amounted to stealing water from one's neighbors. The manipulation of DNA is raising serious moral and scientific questions. But trying to control the business cy-cle has little opposition. After all, who could quarrel with the humanitarian impulse to try and eliminate the pain and suf-fering caused by depressions, the downside of the "boom and bust" cycle. For more than a generation after the New Deal came to Washington, the government worked to con-struct an interlocking web of laws and regulations designed to even out the business cycle. Only in recent years did disen-chantment over Keynesian policies focus on the fact that much of the effort to eliminate the distress of recessions was inflationary. In effect, we didn't really even out the cycle, we simply skewed the trendline upward; each boom was not corrected by a credit contraction, but only interrupted by a pause in inflationary growth.

Economic depressions, like death, are best avoided. However, a study of economic history since ancient times shows that, like death, depressions are not terminal for societies; they are more akin to the cyclical rhythms of our universe such as the rise and fall of the tides, the change of the seasons, and so on. Nevertheless, depressions threaten not only the economic livelihood of politicians, but the immortality ideology of money. Therefore, for nearly 50 years, Americans have been fed a diet of fear about depressions, and the money systems of the world have been engineered to try to support the proposition that progress and prosperity are eternal. Ironically, as with many things, the insistence on perfection is the direct cause of imperfection, and the refusal to accept depressions and recessions as part of the economic landscape and the inability, under the present sociopolitical structure, to establish a steady state economy has set in motion forces that threaten ultimate economic and political collapse. Yet the job of the politician is to survive until the next election and no device is more effective in enabling him to do this than manipulating the nation's money supply.

This is in part because, as we have indicated, in all countries organized along Western lines in the banking business, there is a one-and-a-half to two-year lag between the creation of money and its inflationary effects. For instance, before the presidential election in 1972, there was an extremely sharp rise in the money supply followed two years later by the record inflation of 1974. In the interval, however, the added money stimulated prosperous conditions. The lag effect is widely known among economists and bankers who debate the causes of the increase in the money supply but rarely *understand* it.

The average individual, however, is completely ignorant of this miraculous forecasting tool which enabled International MONEYLINE to predict the 1974 inflation and the return to high double-digit inflation in 1979 and 1980, as well as the decline in the rate of inflation in 1981 and the new inflationary explosion in 1982 and 1983. Because of the tendency of inflation to climb upward to ever higher levels, and because the methods for handling inflation are limited and well-known to government professionals, it is possible to look at the entire decade ahead with a reasonable certainty of what will unfold.

By the time you read this, the world will probably have experienced a severe credit crunch, an international banking crisis, full-scale depression, and final collapse of the dollar with the possibilities for a major war at the end of the decade. However, it will not be the end of the world, and for most people, general conditions won't even be as bad as they were in the 1930s. Because of government's unlimited capacity to create credit (i.e. print money), we will be facing, not a classic price deflation, but an inflationary depression similar to the pattern of 1974, when the Consumer Price Index reached record heights as the economy declined. It will be worse than 1974 and more prolonged. But I believe this environment will provide money-making opportunities for the individual trained in the way of the financial hunter-warrior.

VI

SIMILAR PERIODS OF HISTORY

I am all powerful time which destroys all things, and I have come to slay these men. Even if thou dost not fight, all the warriors facing thee shall die.

Bhagavad Gita

SINCE THE DAWN OF RE-corded history, mankind has experienced alternating periods of feast and famine, of prosperity and depression. Joseph was one of the earliest economists when, according to the Bible, he told the Pharaoh of Egypt that seven years of good harvests would be followed by seven years of poor harvests. In all ages hunters have known periods when game was plentiful and periods when it was not.

Merchants and businessmen have had the same experiences with markets for their goods and services. In economics as in nature, there are cycles of expansion and contraction, some lasting for a few years, others for hundreds of years.

One of the most consistent of these cycles is the half-century cycle called the economic long wave. This consists of roughly 25 years of expansion and 25 years of contraction. Cycles of this duration have been traced back more than 700 years (see chart on the next page) although they show up most clearly over the past 200 years. The year of the French Revolution, 1789, was the trough of a half-century cycle that peaked, as measured by production and prices, in 1814, to be followed by a stock market crash, and depression of the 1820s. The economic decline lasted until the 1840s when economic expansion began again, peaking about 25 years later in 1866, 52 years after the previous peak. The crash and depression came on schedule after the "panic" of 1873, about seven years after the peaking. The U.S. economy continued to contract until the 1890s when a new expansion began. This peaked in 1920 to be followed by the famous crash of 1929 and the depression of the 1930s. Exactly 54 years later in 1974, the economy again peaked and then began the inexorable movement toward breakdown, depression and decline.

That these long waves should be so regular is not so remarkable. The entire universe moves constantly in cycles of expansion and contraction, whether it be the birth or death of a star, or the changing of the seasons, or the personal cycle of birth and death.

Ever since he became a conscious being, man has dreamed of circumventing or defeating these cycles, whether through the development of central heating or air-conditioning, life-preserving medical advances, or religious beliefs in immortality. Applying science and statistical techniques, modern man has also attempted, not only to master the environment of his planet, but also to eliminate the economic cycles of expansion and contraction. The principal tool in this exercise, since the birth of Christ, has been the creation and manipulation of money. But ultimately it never has worked any more than ancient man's rain dances and sacrifices to the corn god brought results.

Artificial stimulation of an economy by money creation— or inflation—always works for a time, but the cyclical economic forces of nature have always prevailed in the end. After the false boom, after the medicine man has been ridiculed or banished, after society has crumbled in its search for an economic fountain of youth, or a computer that will

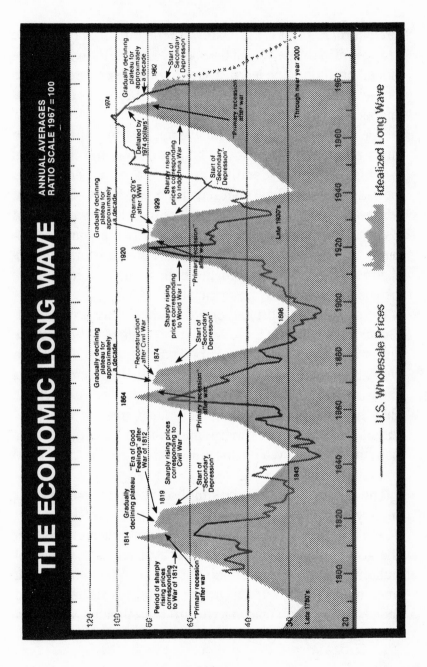

THE ECONOMIC LONG WAVE

ANNUAL AVERAGES
RATIO SCALE 1967 = 100

—— U.S. Wholesale Prices

:::::::: Idealized Long Wave

111

predict markets; it is the shadow of the hunter-warrior who reappears in the psyche of the society and the individual. It is not an attitude to be learned, but to be rediscovered within oneself—the survival heritage of 20 million years—to be summoned forth during "times of trouble."

The tradition of the samurai warrior had its origin in Japan during an extended period of political, economic and social troubles, generally identified as the Tokugawa period. This period, like our own, featured the breakdown of religion, ideals and commercial practices. The individual was thrown back on his inner resources and was drawn toward the ancient hunter-warrior attitudes toward life and survival. Today, as in the Tokugawa era, the civilization in which we live begins to seem phony or artificial.

Corporations report higher profits that really do not exist. Governments report increases in per capita benefits that are really decreases. All the numbers, all the records that you read about in the newspapers, do not seem to describe things the way they really are. Society itself begins to live in what a Buddhist would call "maya," or fantasy, instead of the real world, and one of the primary causes of this is our money and banking system, which fosters what might be called the money illusion.

The money illusion is the simple consequence of creating money by fiat or government order instead of by sweat. There is no longer any legal limit to the amount of money that the government can print. In practical terms that lack of built-in restraint makes endless inflation inevitable. Yet if one understands hunter-warrior strategies as applied to money, there is no reason to regard this situation with fear.

Inflation has plagued the world since the invention of

money. Historically, it was often begun when a king decided that something he wanted to do—such as engage in a costly foreign war—could not be paid for with taxes. If the people were taxed too heavily they would rebel and the king would no longer be able to live out his imperial ambitions. Thus, he chose to pay for his adventures by covertly debasing his subjects' money. The same thing happens in today's world. The recent wave of inflation in the United States started because the government decided to fight an expensive war and at the same time, launch large-scale social programs without raising taxes.

The perennial conservative cry for a balanced budget is simply the demand that the government pay for what it does with tax dollars instead of printing press money. The political problem is that the government often wants to do more than it knows the voters would willingly pay for in taxes. If the government were forced to have a balanced budget, no new programs could be started without cutting back existing ones or asking for new taxes. Obviously, this would greatly limit what the government could do for its citizens and make public life a much less attractive career. Thus, the political answer is always to take the inflation road and pay for things with the "hidden tax" of making everyone's money worth less and less.

The Federal Reserve and the Reagan administration, despite their stated goals of defeating inflation, reducing taxes and balancing the budget, were clearly throwing in the monetary and fiscal towel as the summer of 1982 waned.

The hidden tax of inflation was impossible when trade was based on barter. Try as he might, an ancient king really had no control over the trading value of goatskins or corn or axe

113

heads. The number of pigs that one ox was worth was settled between buyer and seller and it varied with every trade. Inflation had to wait for metal coins to be introduced. Coinage as we think of it appears to have been introduced by the Greeks, who discovered how to stamp coins on both sides toward the end of the 8th century B.C. They were made of a natural mixture of silver and gold called "electrum" and were far more beautifully molded than most coins today. More importantly, their value was easy to see because the coins were stamped according to recognizable standards of weight and fineness *by the governments of the issuing city-state.*

The introduction of standardized coins brought boom times to the Mediterranean area and it is not too difficult to understand why: the more acceptable the medium of exchange, the less haggling required, the greater the number of transactions and the bigger the deals.

By the end of the 7th century B.C., as described by Elgin Groseclose in his book *Money and Man,* it became apparent that the Greeks were in trouble. The increase in coinage had brought prosperity, but it had also brought higher prices. The reason was simply the law of supply and demand. There were more coins in circulation than other commodities and goods, particularly in Athens, where the successful merchants had been exporting and accumulating great hoards of money. Therefore the value of the coins, compared with the value of oxen, axes and slave girls, tended to decline.

To compound the problem, the inventive Greeks not only discovered coinage, they also discovered credit. The vast increase in coinage had brought prosperity, so what could be more logical than to assume that the promise to pay even more coinage at some point in the future—that is, debt— would create even *more* prosperity?

As a result, says Groseclose:

> The greater part of the peasants' holdings had come under mortgage, the evidences of which were stone pillars erected on the land, inscribed . . . with the names of the lender, the amount, the rate, and the maturity of the loan. A still more insidious form of debt was the chattel mortgage—the personal loans known today under soft-sounding phrases like "industrial banking" or "household finance"—by which the farmer could pledge his own person or that of his wife or his children, for the repayment of a loan. These chattels, under Athenian law, could be sold off into slavery, and such was the extent of the existing credit structure that the greater part of the agricultural population was in danger of being converted into bondage.

The famed Solon of Athens came to the rescue with *Seisachtheia,* or "shaking off of burdens." The mortgage pillars were torn down, all agricultural and personal loans were abrogated, and people were forbidden to pledge themselves to possible slavery. The problem of the peasants, the farmers and the small proprietors was solved: they were debt free. However, the *Seisachtheia* nearly ruined the landlords and moneylenders. To help reduce the burden of their debts and the debts of the government, Solon debased the currency by 27 percent. The *mina,* which had formerly consisted of 73 *drachmas,* was made legal tender to the value of 100 *drachmas.* Solon also introduced the interesting practice of charging a fee of 2 percent for minting the coin, *thus reducing the metallic value of the coin below its face value,* and leaving a margin of profit for the state.

In his study of disintegrating civilizations, Arnold Toynbee notes the inflationary effects of the wars of Alexander the Great:

> The mercenaries were paid by putting into circulation the bullion which had been accumulating for two centuries in

the Achaemenian treasuries, and this sudden vast increase in
the value of currency in circulation caused a disastrous inflation in those Greek city-states which had so for been spared
the flail of political strife. Prices soared without any immediate corresponding rise in wages, and this financial
revolution reduced to pauperism the class of peasants and artisans who had hitherto enjoyed a reasonable security.

Originally a military people, the Romans were slow to
begin the use of Greek-style coinage and preferred to settle
debts in bronze and in copper by weight. Military successes
exacted their price, however. Citizens away fighting had to
leave their farms and cattle for long periods. When they
returned, their fields were often in ruin and they had to bor-
row money to rebuild, or simply to live. Eventually, the
burden of debt became as crushing as it had been during the
time of Solon, and the Romans adopted the "Greek Solution"
—massive debt cancellations. At the same time the military
victories of the legions brought a huge inflow of booty for the
generals, tribute payments and proconsular revenues, and a
flood of imports, mostly from conquered Eastern countries.

The predictable result: roaring inflation.

Rome was the *great creditor nation.* It became the center of
world finance and banking. There was even a stock market
similar to that of the U.S. in the 1960s, and senators, noblemen and commoners alike bought and sold shares in companies which had tax collecting privileges in various foreign
provinces. Some speculators became wealthy. Others went
broke. There were periods of enormous prosperity and
periodic panics. Rome was the prototype of what was to
become the typical inflationary society. And, as is character-
istic of such societies, the great accumulation of wealth was
not used to reduce government debt. Partly because of infla-

tion and partly because of the huge expense of maintaining a world empire—such as the exhausting 20-year war with Carthage—the costs of government increased astoundingly.

To meet these costs and to compensate the moneylenders and bankers for their losses from the debt cancellations, the Romans took another leaf from the Book of Solon: they depreciated the currency.

The first really significant depreciation took place after the Punic wars with Carthage. The *as*, the oldest Roman monetary unit, which originally represented one pound of copper, had its value cut in half, from four ounces to two ounces, by the middle of the 3rd century. By 89 B.C., just before it was eliminated from circulation, it had been reduced to a half ounce of copper.

The accession of Nero (A.D. 54) marked the beginning of a long series of further currency debasements. The dramatic progression of this process can be traced by following the decline in the *denarius* as shown in the following table:

Issuer	% Silver
Nero, A.D. 54	94
Vitellius, A.D. 68	81
Domitian, A.D. 81	92
Trajan, A.D. 98	93
Hadrian, A.D. 117	87
Antoninus Pius, A.D. 138	75
Marcus Aurelius, A.D. 161	68
Septimus Severus, A.D. 193	50
Elaganbalus, A.D. 218	43
Alexander Severus, A.D. 222	35
Gordian, A.D. 238	28
Philip, A.D. 244	0.5
Claudius Gothicus, A.D. 268	0.02

The reductions in silver content fluctuated until A.D. 98. Then the reductions started accelerating; each time a larger percentage was removed. During this entire period, Rome was a great and powerful empire, continuing to rule most of the known world. The barbarian invasion did not begin until about 100 years after Claudius, and the Sack of Rome, which marked the beginning of the end of the empire, did not take place until A.D. 408.[1] As George Finlay reports:

> In reviewing the causes which contributed to the decline of the wealth and diminution of the population of the Roman Empire it is necessary to take into account the depreciation of the coinage which frequently robbed large classes of the industrious citizens of a great part of their wealth, reduced the value of property, produced confusion in legal contracts, and anarchy in prices in public markets. The evils which must have resulted from the enormous depreciation of the Roman coinage at several periods can only be understood by a chronological record of the principal changes, and by remembering that each issue of a depreciated coinage was an act of bankruptcy on the part of the reigning emperor.
>
> [George Finlay, *History of Greece*, 1851]

By the reign of Septimus Severus in A.D. 193, it is reported that distrust in the value of money began interfering with foreign commercial aid and, increasingly, only gold was accepted. However, gold coins were also debased, sometimes by as much as 50 percent. Since impurities in gold coins are easier to detect, they held their value more stubbornly than the rest.

By the end of the 4th century A.D., traders were very reluctant to accept any coin at face value. In most business

---

[1] The eastern half of the Roman Empire, whose capital city was Constantinople, did not devalue its currency—the *bezant* kept exactly the same metallic weight and fineness for 800 years—and this half of the empire lasted another 1000 years.

transactions, it became necessary to assay and weigh each piece. This slowed down the number of transactions and eroded the foundations of credit.

The clock of commerce was turned back. Barter again became the only way of carrying out most transactions. The entire emerging apparatus of trade, which had risen on the Greek idea of universally acceptable money, began to disintegrate. Business stagnated, land went untilled, government treasuries remained empty and grass began to grow between the cobblestones of the vast network of Roman roads that knit the empire together. Wealthy families turned all their worldly possessions into precious metals or jewelry and buried it in the grounds of their great estates against the day of inevitable collapse. Meanwhile, the emperors put on the famed Roman circuses in an effort to keep an increasingly poor population under control. "By the seventh century," says Groseclose:

> the weights themselves (used to determine the metallic content of money) had been so frequently degraded that it was no longer possible to make a specific bargain for money. There was no law to define the weight of a pound or an ounce, and no power to enforce the law if one existed. Under these circumstances, money became extinct. Nor, are we reminded, was it the only institution that perished; all institutions had perished.

The fall of the Roman Empire marked the beginning of what is known as the Dark Ages. In the conventional history books, which most of us studied as youngsters, we learned that the "fall" was due mainly to the "high living" of the Romans after they had conquered the world, and to the increasingly savage attacks of the barbarians. The barbarians, in fact, are given most of the blame for setting back the clock on the progress of civilization. Yet when we reexamine this period through a numismatic lens, it becomes clear that the destruction of money and money standards played a significant role in driving society back into a primitive state. More specifically, it was a lack of full understanding of:

▶ 1. The inflationary impact of increasing the supply of money, regardless of its standard of valuation.

▶ 2. The inflationary effects of continued depreciation of money by reducing the actual value of the coinage, or its supporting value, to less than the face value of the money.

▶ 3. The use of money to divert real purchasing power to the essentially destructive activities of war, which tended to *reduce* real wealth.

Roberto Vacca, in his book, *The Coming Dark Age*, published in 1973, projects a complete breakdown in the entire technological system that supports modern civilization: transportation, electrical power, postal service, garbage collection, and so forth. It will happen, he believes, because the exponential growth rates of world population, energy consumption and requirements for other facilities become greater than the capacity of the civilization to pay for them with real money, which is productivity transformed into purchasing power. Any other kind of money—fiat money or "funny money"—is a myth that can only lead to an economic nightmare.

It is interesting to observe that, as we approach what Vacca describes as the "knee" of the dangerous exponential upward growth curve from which the collapse is projected, we find the condition of the world money systems very similar to those existing during the time of the Roman Empire. In any event, as we pick our way through the further history of inflation into modern times, it would be well to remember the words of one old Roman, Antoninus Augustus: "Money had more to do with the distemper of the Roman Empire than the Huns or the Vandals."

Inflation, almost invariably associated with an excess of paper money, is the result of an excess of money of any kind. Nowhere is this more clearly demonstrated than in the first great modern inflation that was the direct result of the acquisition of vast hoards of gold by the Spanish Conquistadores, Cortes in Mexico, Pizarro in Peru and Almagro in Chile.

The Spanish soldiers were the best in the world. For 150 years after the discovery of America, they never lost a battle, in Europe or the New World. In addition to being dedicated to spreading the word of God to the heathen, they had a maniacal greed for gold, which they looted from the Aztec and Inca treasuries and beat out of Indian slave laborers in the American mines.

Between 1503 and 1660, total gold and silver imports from America were around $2.5 billion—a lot of money in those days. However, as the golden stream poured into Spain and spread through Europe, bringing a sharp expansion of trade and prosperity, the gold itself began to lose value. No longer scarce, it was not as valuable as it had been before the discovery of the Americas, and the prices of everything else quickly doubled.

At the pinnacle of its power, with its fighting men undefeated and the lion's share of the world gold supply,

Spain was not too concerned about inflation. The Spanish kings were interested in expanding the scope of their power and dominating the world.

The result was a series of costly wars against France, Germany, the Netherlands and even the Vatican, which eventually bankrupted the seemingly inexhaustible Spanish treasury.

Under Philip II (1556–98) the decline began. The country drifted into the hands of the moneylenders, who charged exorbitant interest rates and reaped enormous profits at the expense of the state.

In 1575, the crash came. The government was out of money and the moneylenders would extend no more credit. So the government suspended grants of royal revenue and issued the famous "Second Decree," which reduced all interest rates throughout the empire to 5 percent.

The result was the financial ruin of the big money centers at Antwerp and Genoa and a collapse of trade and commerce in every important city in Europe. Unpaid for months, the Spanish garrison at Antwerp sacked the city with unbelievable ferocity. Food shortages, riots and general unrest spread from country to country. Then, in 1603, Philip III, in a replay of the ancient and time-tested scenario, debased the currency. The old copper *vellon* which was all that remained in general circulation, was restamped at double its previous face value.

In *The Golden Century of Spain,* R. Trevor Davies vividly describes life after the crash in Spain:

> Soon after the end of Philip III's reign, gold and silver had virtually disappeared everywhere. All payments great and small had to be made in copper with the result that great

wagons and numerous porters were necessary for the trans-
ference of comparatively small sums. The money paid for
wax candles would weigh nearly three times as much as the
candles . . . . The majority of Spaniards became idlers; it
makes one pause and think to see all the streets of Madrid full
of idlers and vagabonds playing cards all day long.

Thus did hubris and inflation bring down one of the first great
modern empires of the Western world.

Meanwhile, in England, in 1545, usury was legalized by
Henry VIII, and a great new financial idea swept through the
capitals of Europe: financing through debt.

Because of the Church ban on interest, in effect almost
since the fall of Rome, there was no advantage in lending
money except, of course, for interest paid under the table.
When Henry VIII set a legal limit of 10 percent, the money
began to come out of the coffers and the people who grasped
the idea best were the English goldsmiths.

Long used to keeping gold and other precious metals on
deposit for their customers, the goldsmiths gave out receipts.
The receipts were passed from hand to hand in business
transactions, behaving as money, while the gold remained on
deposit. Naturally, it was not long before some goldsmiths
got the bright idea of lending out some of the gold they were
holding at interest. At the time it was an extremely daring
idea. After all, one was attempting to profit by lending someone else's money. It was so profitable and useful to governments and entrepreneurs alike that the experiment became
the basis for modern banking.

The goldsmiths discovered that once people became used
to the idea of leaving their gold on deposit and accepting
paper notes, there were very few calls for delivery of gold at
any one time. Thus, it was possible to extend credit to people

far in excess of the actual gold or silver coins on deposit. A certain percentage of the deposits were kept in reserve—that is, not lent—to meet withdrawal demands.

The same reserve system is used in the United States today. Thus, from an initial deposit of $5,000 and a 20 percent "reserve" (the present reserve figure for most large banks is 18 percent) of, say $1,000, a bank is able to lend out $4,000. This money is, in turn, deposited in the same or another bank, where $800 is kept as a "reserve" and $3,200 is lent out. At the third bank, assuming the money is deposited, $640 is kept in reserve and the balance is lent, and so on until the original $5,000 is multiplied to $25,000 or more in the case of some smaller banks, which have lower requirements. The Monetary Control Act of 1980 has reduced reserve requirements significantly below these levels—making possible an increase of the money supply by as much as an additional 300 percent and thus setting the stage for further inflationary explosions.

Where does all this money come from? It's simply credit— that is, money created out of thin air by rotation through the commercial banking system.

The man who first saw the fantastic possibilities of what might be called the "goldsmith principle" was, logically enough, the son of a goldsmith, John Law. Law was born a Scot and, in complete violation of the penurious traditions of the Scottish, was a playboy. After running through the family fortune shortly after the turn of the 18th century, he was forced to flee the country because he had killed a man in a duel. Several years later, he turned up in France as a partner of a young French nobleman who liked to tour the Parisian gambling halls. After Louis XIV died and his nobleman friend became prince regent, Law decided his true calling was high finance.

What Law had in mind was to apply the goldsmith principle to the problems of France, then in deep trouble because of the large war debts run up by Louis XIV. Law wanted to issue notes, 25 percent backed by gold and silver, and 75 percent supported by debt obligations of the French government. Initially, he proposed that the notes issued would be convertible at sight into gold or silver. The underlying idea was to replace the old money, that is gold and silver, with a new kind of money that simply consisted of stamped pieces of paper that could be run off on a printing press.

It was the implementation of this concept in France on the 5th of May 1716, which marked the beginning of the modern inflationary age. It was also the first case of government debt obligations being used to create money—a practice that is standard for the U.S. Treasury and the Federal Reserve today.

At the time Law put his 25/75 plan into effect, government bonds, or *billet d'état* as they were called, were selling at a discount of 78½% because no one thought they ever would be paid. Much to the surprise of everybody, the notes issued by Law, which were backed by the nearly worthless government bonds, began to sell at a 1% premium.

You don't have to be an expert in finance to figure out what happened. The Regent concluded that if you could create $30 million out of $7½ million worth of gold and silver and old government paper, then why not try for $60 million? Law's bank was granted a charter as the Banque Générale and, in the next four years, the equivalent of about $5 billion in paper currency was printed. The country experienced the greatest prosperity in its history. Prices skyrocketed, but it didn't matter because everyone had money.

It became increasingly obvious that if everyone went to the Banque Générale and asked for silver and gold in return for their paper money, they would not be able to get it, so a few of the more cynical and suspicious characters quietly converted their paper money into gold and silver.

One of the wealthiest and most important men of the time, the Prince de Conti, decided to convert all his money. When word of this reached the regent, he was furious. He ordered the prince to put the gold and silver back immediately, but word of de Conti's action spread and other people started doing the only sensible thing—withdrawing more gold and silver. Soon, precious metals were disappearing so fast that Law had only one alternative—to refuse to convert the paper into metal at all and, eventually, to outlaw silver and gold. Under penalty of a heavy fine and confiscation, any individual was forbidden to hold more than a specific amount of coinage.

None of the measures worked. Legal or not, the coin of the realm in most transactions was still coin. People were reluctant to part with their hidden gold and silver, and no one would accept the now totally worthless paper money.

After the John Law experience, one would have thought that the French would be cured of further experimentation with inflation. However, even in the 18th century, the demand for increased public expenditures without matching taxation put continuous pressure on French monetary and fiscal policies.

This period in France was an era of rising expectations. Increasing industrialization and expanded commerce broke down the old social structure that had prevailed under feudalism. The noblemen on the great estates found themselves losing power to the merchants of the town, and, in an effort to regain that power, they put increased pressure to produce on the peasants. But the peasants' eyes had been opened by increased communications and employment opportunities in the cities. Their lot had been improving steadily and they dreamed of more. Many of them became shopkeepers and artisans—a group later referred to as the "petite bourgeoisie."

All Frenchmen were living in an era in which "things were changing" and many classes of society were achieving a higher standard of living.

But, because of unsettled political conditions following the first phase of the revolution, there was a general lack of confidence among merchants and businessmen. Capital, the lifeblood of expansion, had retreated underground, and the government, unable to increase taxes, sank deeper into debt.

The money experts thought that the solution was an increase in the "circulating medium," or money supply. More money, it was argued, would stimulate increased trade and, eventually, prosperity.

By money, of course, they meant printed pieces of paper, since there didn't seem to be any way to obtain large quantities of metallic currencies. The new money was not to be the worthless paper of John Law. This time each *assignat*, as the money came to be called, would be backed by that most solid asset of all, land.

Henry VIII had seized church lands in England and his successors, Elizabeth I and James I, had sold them off to raise money for the government. So it did not even seem to be particularly revolutionary for the government to seize all the church lands in France, and use them as backing for the new issue of paper money.

Initially, some 400 million *livres*, or *assignats*, were issued, " . . . secured by a pledge of productive real estate and bearing interest at 3 percent." As Andrew Dickson White writes in *Fiat Money Inflation in France:*

> To stimulate loyalty, the portrait of the king was placed in the center; to arouse public spirit, patriotic legends and emblems surrounded it; to stimulate public cupidity, the amount of interest which the note would yield each day to the holder was printed in the margin; and the whole was duly garnished with stamps and signatures to show that it was carefully registered and controlled.
>
> The National Assembly declared: "Paper money is without inherent value unless it represents some special property. Without representing some special property, it is inadmissible in trade to compete with a metallic currency, which has a value real and is independent of the public action; therefore it is that the paper money which has only the public authority as its basis has always caused ruin where it has been established; that is the reason why the bank notes of 1720 issued by John Law, after having caused terrible evils, have left only frightful memories.
>
> Therefore, it is that the National Assembly has not wished to expose you to this danger, but has given this new paper money not only a value derived from the national authority, but a value real and immutable, a value which permits it to sustain advantageously a competition with the precious metals themselves."

The declaration added: "These *assignats,* bearing interest as they do, will soon be considered better than the coin now hoarded, and will bring it out again into circulation."

It was quickly suggested that sufficient *assignats* ought to be issued to cover the entire national debt of France. At the same time, it was proposed that while the *assignats* would be convertible to land, the land could not be sold for gold or silver. It was predicted that gold would lose all its value.

Soon, the total number of *assignats* was increased to 800 million, but the National Assembly stipulated that the total amount put into circulation could under no circumstances exceed 1,200 million. At the same time, it was provided that as fast as the *assignats* were paid into the treasury for land they would be burned. Thus, a healthy contraction of the money supply could be maintained. In addition, the later issues were to bear no interest.

Within a short time, 160 million *assignats* were exchanged for land, but they were not retired as promised. Instead, they were reissued and rapidly began to lose value. But the depreciation was easily "explained": the Bourbon family was in some mysterious way drawing all the metallic money out of the country, the depreciation was due to the fact that greedy businessmen were raising prices, British agents were spreading propaganda about the worthlessness of paper money. There was even what sounded like a fairly modern argument by the famous diplomat, Talleyrand: imports were too great and exports too small. In any event, there was an accelerated flow of hard money out of the country.

Heavy duties were placed on foreign goods. Increasingly severe penalties were imposed for dealing in silver and gold. Finally, on September 8, 1793, the penalty for anyone refusing to accept *assignats*, or for accepting them at a discount, was death, with confiscation of the criminal's property. Rewards were offered to anyone informing the authorities of criminal transactions.

Business was stimulated. The number of transactions involving various forms of property and goods grew to frenetic levels, and the velocity of the circulation of the *assignats*—a classic phenomenon of all inflationary periods—accelerated. All of this was largely due to increasing flight from paper currency into tangibles: from buildings and machines to artworks, antiques and even such commodities as corn and wheat.

An illusion of prosperity was created—what Andrew Dickson White has called the "law of accelerating issue and depreciation"—that began to assert itself. To sustain the illusion, larger issues of *assignats* were needed. By 1796 more than 45 billion *assignats* had been issued—19 times the original national debt. Yet people continued to complain about a "shortage of money."

It is difficult to this day for many to understand why the money backed by and convertible into land failed. To begin with, most people could not afford to convert their money into land. They needed the money for other purposes, such as food, clothing and shelter. But the root reason for the collapse of money values was that increasing the quantity of money, *by itself,* does not create lasting prosperity. In fact, as we have seen since Roman times, *an increase in the quantity of money— even when it is gold and silver—leads to a decline in the real value of that money.* For its only real value is its measurement in terms of the other goods and services it can buy and the growth of real wealth, as represented by property, equipment, goods or other material objects which in themselves have value regardless of the money standard used to measure them.

One of the clearest proofs of the importance of the quantity of money was the fact that, throughout the revolutionary

period in France, the original *assignats,* which carried a por-
trait of the king, continued to have a much higher value than
subsequent issues. After the king was beheaded, no more
such notes were printed, and there was a greater scarcity of
them. This odd phenomenon was repeated during the inflation after the Russian Revolution in 1917, when currency
bearing the head of the czar, intrinsically worth nothing at all
and publicly repudiated, bought more goods than official
currency printed by the communist government.

Many techniques were tried to stop the depreciation of the
assignats, such as trying to get people to convert them into 5
percent government bonds. Also tried was a plan that today
would be called indexation, much discussed throughout the
Western world in 1974 as a cure-all for hyperinflation. In
France, in 1974, it was called the "scale of proportion." It
meant that the amount of a debt was proportionately increased with each new issue of paper money. If I owed you
24 *assignats* when the first issue took place, the amount
would have been increased to 456 by the time of the final
issue, assuming, of course, that the "scale of proportion" had
been working during the entire period.

This system did not work, because the *rate of the depreciation of the money was not uniform.* During a period of hyperinflation, prices are like race horses. Some move rapidly
ahead, while others slip behind; traditionally comparable
standards of value become distorted. Each new issue of
money is like a wave washing up on a shallow beach, highest
at the place where it first strikes the shore and lower at every
point thereafter until the last of it disappears as a fleck of foam
soaking into the sand. France increasingly became a nation of
debtors, and the debtors became the advocates of an increas-

ing number of money waves as a method by which their debts could be wiped out.

Ultimately, the revolutionary government resorted to the same solution that had been applied by their Roman forebears: new money, to be called *mandat,* backed by only the choicest real estate that would be "good as gold." Unfortunately, the experts failed to realize that at any point any association of money with real estate would make it suspect to the public. It was only a few months before the *mandat* was no better than the *assignat.*

The expression "man on a white horse" comes from the takeover of the French Government by Napoleon after the failure of the *mandat* had brought total economic stagnation and social chaos.

No sooner had he been appointed First Consul of France than the ministers and financial experts flocked to his quarters demanding to know what he would do about monetary and fiscal policy. The government was bankrupt and deeply in debt. Enemy armies were attacking on two fronts, and civil war was threatening. The French armies were unpaid. The largest loan that could be raised was sufficient only to run the government for a single day. What would be his policy?

"I will pay cash (gold) or I will pay nothing," Napoleon said.

The American Revolution was conceived in inflation and dedicated to the proposition that it was possible to fight a war for independence without paying for it. Avoiding payment for wars has been an American tradition. In 1776, it seemed eminently logical, since the whole point of the revolution was to avoid unjust British taxation. To levy taxes to pay soldiers to lay down their lives to prevent taxes seemed inconsistent.

A number of Continental congressmen appeared to understand the consequences of inflation very well. In a resolution of Congress in 1777, it was declared:

> No truth being more evident than that, where the quantity of money of any denomination exceeds what is useful as a medium of commerce, its comparative value must be proportionately reduced.

Nevertheless, they decided that the member states would issue "anticipations" in proportion to the estimated population of each state. The paper was backed by the "full faith and credit" of the colonies. It was called anticipations, because it was anticipated that some day Congress would levy taxes in silver or gold which would be used to redeem the paper notes.

Revolutionary monetary expert Pelatiah Webster declared at the time that "the value of the current money in any country cannot be increased by an action made to its quantity." However, he added, according to William Graham Sumner in his *The Finances and the Financier of the American Revolution,* that "no State can be ruined or much endangered by any debt due to itself only." A century and a half later, when President Roosevelt was pressed by conservative critics of the growing national debt, he liked to reduce them to speechless rage with the offhand comment that the debt was nothing to worry about because "we owe it to ourselves."

And so the printing presses began to roll. According to Sumner:

> The amount of Continental Currency issued in 1775 was $6 million; in 1776, $19 million; in 1777, $13 million; in 1778, $63 million. The "dollars" were the Spanish milled silver

dollars which were the primary circulating coins in the colonies. Initially, as in the case of the French Revolution thirteen years later, the paper money seemed to work miracles. Benjamin Franklin, who was the American Ambassador to France, wrote in a letter from Paris: "This currency, as we manage it, is a wonderful machine. It performs its office when we issue it; it pays and clothes troops, and provides victuals and ammunition, and when we are obliged to issue a quantity excessive, it pays itself off by depreciation."

The only problem was that the depreciation drove the Spanish dollar out of circulation, or used it up to pay for foreign imports. Prices soared and credit disappeared. As Sumner noted, "Who would become a lender on a depreciating currency?"

Prices of food and clothing doubled within a year and Congress resorted to "forced circulation." It was resolved: "That said bills (Continental dollars) ought to be equal to Spanish dollars, and whoever shall ask, offer, or receive more in said bills for gold, silver, houses or goods than of any other kind of money, or shall refuse to receive such bills for goods ought to be deemed an enemy and forfeit the value of the money or goods, or house and lands."

Price controls were introduced along with the death penalty for counterfeiting, a crime made easy because the paper money was poorly made. In Massachusetts, a convention was called for the purpose of finding out the cause of high prices and establishing a system for punishing the greedy. As always, price control immediately produced shortages. In 1779, a writer in Boston observed:

The miseries of famine are now mingled with the horrors of war. The poor people in the almshouses have been destitute of grain and other necessaries these many days. Many reputable families are almost starving.

In March, 1780, Congress took the standard step: it introduced an entirely new system of currency. According to the new act:

> the States were to bring in their quotas monthly, as heretofore provided for twelve months, silver and gold being taken at the rate of one to forty. All bills which came in this way were to be destroyed, and other bills were to be issued for not more than one twentieth of those destroyed, to be redeemable in specie within six years and to bear interest at five percent in specie, payable at the redemption of the bills. [The International Monetary Fund had a similar idea in 1973 when it was decided to pay interest of five percent on the SDRs or "paper gold" issued by the fund.]

The new currency fared no better than the old and depreciated by half by the end of summer. Finally, by the Act of March 18, 1780, Congress abandoned all hope of ever paying the notes and declared itself bankrupt. Meanwhile, George Washington and his unpaid soldiers were continuing to refuse to give in to the British redcoats, providing further proof that it was possible to fight a war for independence without paying for it—at least for a while.

Ultimately, it became clear that, unless something was done, the American revolutionaries might literally "all hang together." Benjamin Franklin used his great powers of persuasion to raise several hundred thousand dollars in France as an advance from the French monarchy, which was, in turn, bankrupting itself trying to defeat England. Ironically, the same monarchy would be overthrown during the inflation of the French Revolution less than a decade later.

At the same time, who should enter the American revolutionary stage but an American version of John Law, one Robert Morris of Philadelphia, who, as Sumner says, was "the only man in the history of the world who ever bore the title of Superintendent of Finance." Morris was a merchant and speculator who reportedly had made a fortune from financing privateers to plunder the British sea trade. Morris was 41 when the revolution began and well connected with the various revolutionary groups of Philadelphia.

In 1781, shortly after being appointed to his new office, he submitted a plan to Congress for bringing the hard-pressed rebels out of their financial difficulties. Said Morris: "This country by relying too much on paper is in a condition of peculiar disorder and debility." The solution he proposed was raising money from France and establishing a national bank which he said would become a "pillar of American credit." Demonstrating as shrewd an understanding of the "goldsmith principle" as John Law himself, he stated:

> When once by punctual payment the notes of the bank have obtained full credit, the sum in specie which will be deposited will be such that *the bank will have the interest of a stock two or three times larger than that which it really possesses.*

Explaining further, he said the main reason for the bank is:

> that the small sums advanced by the holders of bank stock may be multiplied in the usual manner by means of their credit, so as to increase the resource which the government can draw from it and, at the same time, by placing the collective mass of private credit between the lenders and borrowers, supply at once the want of ability on the one hand, and of credit on the other.

The bank began business January 7, 1782, and was an immediate success. Government bills were paid, troops were regularly fed and clothed, embargoes and other restrictions were removed and the economy began to take on a semblance of normalcy. Although Morris faced a constant

136

series of problems in financing the American cause he was able to write in a private letter in 1784: "The only money now in general circulation is specie and notes from the American bank, which have the same credit as silver."

All was not sweetness and light, however. One writer quoted by Sumner says that when people went to the bank to get silver:

> they found a display of silver on the counter and men employed in raising boxes containing silver, or supposed to contain silver, from the cellar into the banking room, or lowering them from the banking room into the cellar. By contrivances like these, the bank obtained the reputation of possessing immense wealth; but its hollowness was several times nearly made apparent, especially on one occasion when one of the co-partners withdrew a deposit of some $5 or $6 thousand when the whole species of the bank did not exceed $20 thousand.

It was further alleged that Morris kept the silver and paid the revolutionary soldiers in notes "with which they purchased shoes at ten dollars a pair." Nevertheless, Morris went forward with the establishment of a Continental Mint and retired from office only after the Constitution had been drafted specifically prohibiting the government from ever again issuing paper money as legal tender.

An interesting relic of the inflationary period of the American Revolution is Article I, Section 10 of the Constitution that says, in part, "No State shall make anything but gold and silver coin a tender in payment of debts." The article wasn't set aside until the need arose to fight another war on the cuff.

Despite the disastrous experiences with paper money in France and the United States in the 18th century, its use—and abuse—continued. In the United States, in the early part of the 19th century, paper money continued to exercise a fatal fascination. And since there was no central control of note issue or uniform regulation, it wasn't long before a "frenzy of paper inflation" began to sweep the country. Banks were formed in remote places, so their notes could be presented in exchange for coin only with great difficulty. Some notes sold at a substantial discount. In New York, they were referred to as "red dog" and "wild cat" currency. Alabama created a state bank and began printing money backed by "the faith and credit and wealth of the state." In the panic of 1837 it was found that some $6 million of the bank's assets were worthless and the system collapsed. A state bank was established in Mississippi and the pattern repeated itself on an even larger scale. As one observer of the time described it: "The $48 million of the bank's loans were never paid: the $23 million of notes and deposits were never redeemed. The whole system fell, in a huge and shapeless wreck, leaving the people of the state very much as they came into the world. Everybody was in debt without any possible means of payment. . . . Lands became worthless, for the reason that no one had any money to pay for them." It should be noted that this episode took place during the downswing of an economic long wave, providing some evidence that money printing cannot reverse major economic tides.

These catastrophic experiments ended with the establishment of a national banking system in 1863–64, which introduced centralized control of private money. The purpose of the banking act was not to provide the nation with sound money, but to aid the federal government in financing the Civil War. In other words it was another inflationary solution.

When the Civil War began, the national government was deeply in debt and nearly unable to raise money. Only $7 million of a $10 million Treasury issue was subscribed and the government was forced to pay interest rates as high as 36 percent.

The white knight in this situation was Salmon P. Chase, Lincoln's Secretary of the Treasury. Chase was known as a "hard money man" of the old school. However, he decided the best way to finance the war was in the 1776 tradition—on credit. The Confederacy had the same idea and soon the Southern states were flooded with what became nearly worthless paper currency.

In the North, problems began to develop when the banks undertook to lend the government $150 million in four months when they had an aggregate capitol of only $120 million and combined coin reserves of only $63 million. The plan was to lend the coin to the government in return for government securities which would be resold to the public to bring the coin back into the banks. The plan broke down in mid-passage and payments in coin had to be suspended. On the same day, it was proposed in Congress that the United States resort to the issue of irredeemable paper currency which later became the infamous greenbacks.

The debate in Congress was hot and heavy. As reported by Wesley Mitchell in his *History of the Greenbacks,* a congressman named Lovejoy declared:

> It is not in the power of this Congress . . . to accomplish an impossibility in making something out of nothing. The piece of paper you stamp at five dollars is not five dollars, and it never will be unless it is convertible into a five dollar gold piece; and to profess that it is, is simply a delusion and a fallacy.

Nevertheless, the Legal Tender Bill (later declared unconstitutional) was passed, calling for the issuance of $150 million in greenbacks. It was, of course, generally agreed that there would be no further issues, but by 1864, $449 million in greenbacks had been issued. This amount was reduced to $336 million in 1867, and then increased again to $382 million in 1873–74. Finally in 1879, after what was regarded as the most severe depression in U.S. history up to that time, the greenbacks were retired and payment of coin resumed.

Thus, for a period of 17 years, the country functioned with a paper currency that was inconvertible. For the monetary student it was a particularly interesting period of American history because in some ways it approximates our own. Gold was officially reduced to the status of being "a commodity," and there were free-floating foreign exchange rates between the U.S. and other countries.

A number of U.S. securities required payment in gold, and gold was used as bank reserves and in various special transactions. However, there was no legally fixed ratio between gold and the greenbacks. As Milton Friedman points out in his *Monetary History of the United States,* the country was really on a dual monetary standard of the greenback dollar and the gold dollar, one official and the other unofficial.

Almost immediately following the issues of greenbacks, the country was hit with a booming inflation. The greenback price of gold doubled in less than two years. The silver coinage—dimes, quarters, etc.—became worth more than the paper currency and soon began to disappear from circulation for melting or hoarding. The government was forced to issue paper "change" which became known as "shinplasters."

Businessmen generally did well, and salaried individuals

and those living on fixed incomes suffered. A substantial percentage of the population was still agricultural and the suffering was considerably less than during later inflationary periods.

A good capsule is provided in the 1865 report of Hugh McCullough, U.S. Secretary of the Treasury:

> There are no indications of real and permanent prosperity . . . in the splendid fortunes reported to be made by skillful manipulations at the gold room, or the stock board; no evidence of increasing wealth in the facts that railroads and steamboats are crowded with passengers, and hotels with guests; that cities are full to overflowing, and rents and the necessities of life, as well as luxuries, are daily advancing. All these things prove rather . . . that the number of *non-producers is increasing, and that productive industry is being diminished.* There is no fact more manifest than that the plethora of paper money is not only undermining the morals of the people by encouraging waste and extravagance, but is striking at the root of our material prosperity by diminishing labor.

It is worth noting that all of this took place at the peak of an economic long wave similar to that of 1973–74—and the consequences were the same.

Subsequently, the country went back to the conversion of paper money into gold, but not until after the financial panic of 1873 and subsequent great depression of the 1870s. Additional greenbacks were issued in 1873–74 in an effort to provide "easy money," but they did little good, and the country returned to a silver and gold standard—that is, paper money was redeemable in gold at the bank—in 1879. While there was some economic recovery, the major downswing phase of the long wave, as shown in the economic long wave chart, continued until the 1890s.

Our current economy has far more sophisticated methods

of control than in former times. However, as we have seen, wage and price controls, indexation, easy money, and a return to sound money all have been tried before and have not worked.

Thus the message for the hunter-warrior is clear: deal with the world as it is, not as public officials tell you it is, or as you would like it to be. Whether there is genuine deflation or more inflation, the economic winter is upon us, and game will be more scarce. Therefore, hunt more carefully, conserve your personal energies, and keep reserves that can be translated easily into purchasing power.

VII
AI UCHI!*

Be a warrior and kill desire, the powerful
enemy of the soul.

Bhagavad Gita

*Cut your opponent before he cuts you.

N OW THAT WE HAVE

a historic picture of the cyclical patterns of economies under inflationary stress, what can the individual do? How can you apply hunter-warrior thinking to the present and anticipated economic situation?

The hunter-warrior is very much aware of the seasons and plans his strategy accordingly. For instance, snow means he can follow tracks much more easily, but he must deal with cold. Some animals can be hunted more easily in one season than in another, and this is also true of markets. No hunter would hope for a change in the seasons; he would simply adapt to conditions—and that is what modern traders and investors should do. Numerous studies of long economic cycles show that there have been alternate periods of expansion and contraction throughout history, much as there are changes in the seasons. Booms always wind down to be replaced by hard times that, in turn, end, to begin a new boom. These economic tides have been ebbing and flowing throughout recorded history, despite a government's capacity to create money.

Therefore, what is important in the final analysis is the ability of the individual to understand and cope with the circumstances that prevail. Perhaps the greatest enemy you will face in financial markets is not fake or misleading public statements, or the players on the other side of the table, but yourself. Your desire to be always right, your dream of making a killing, your greed for more.

That is why the *Bhagavad Gita,* one of the most ancient Sanskrit texts, written before the birth of the Buddha about 500 B.C., advises: "Be a warrior and kill desire, the powerful enemy of the soul." For it is only by raising your consciousness beyond the usual feelings of greed and fear that you can achieve clarity—whether in the battle of war or the battle for investment survival. To the hunter-warrior, greed is not only personally damaging, it is threatening to his world environment.

For example, echoing the advice of expert hunters through the centuries, Elmer Keith, in *Guns and Ammo for Hunting Big Game,* advises, "Kill only such game as you want for meat and trophy, then take time to properly preserve what you do kill and many head of game will be left in the hills for posterity. You will have a better trip by so doing and feel that you have not wasted the game." For the trader or investor, this translates into never trying to buy at the low or trying to get the last dollar of profit.

The result of clarity is more realistic analysis and decisions. The financial warrior assesses the basic conditions as they are—not as he would like them to be—and then makes his hunting plan accordingly. For instance, the automobile business was one of the great building blocks of American business. But in the early 1980s, Detroit was not a good place to go hunting for a job. On the other hand, food is a basic necessity. Therefore, as the world population grows and starvation spreads, farming may again become a highly profitable business.

The financial warrior never falls in love with his investment. When real interest rates are high, he keeps his money in government money funds. When the Federal Reserve accelerates money printing, creating excess financial liquidity, he keeps stocks, and when the rate of inflation starts to accelerate, he buys gold. If you lose your job, make use of adversity as the hunter might use a rainy day to repair weapons, to increase your education or skills even if it is no more than to read at home.

The history of the economic long wave shows that the United States is moving into an extended period of economic decline that will be all the more uncomfortable because it's likely to be accompanied by inflation. In short, you may well face what would seem to be the worst of both worlds: a sharp rise in unemployment, a decline in business activity, a drop in take-home pay, and continued high and rising prices. In other words, an inflationary depression. For a time there will be bankruptcies, layoffs, and a heavier debt load on both the nation and the individual. But then that dread enemy of our society, inflation, will seemingly come to the rescue—only to become the enemy again.

As we have said, the reason for this is simple: since the 1930s no Western nation has been willing to let the excesses of a boom be washed out by a full-scale bust. The pain of deflation has simply become politically unacceptable. Any democratically elected official that tried to go through with it would simply be voted out of office. Thus the solution to inflation has almost universally become monetary reflation followed by a resort to wage-and-price controls, an economic band-aid that seems to help for a while, but which does nothing to cure the underlying malady.

Thus we assume that as soon as depression gets too painful

in terms of unemployment, the administration in Washington—whether Republican or Democratic—will try to cure it by taking the inflationary road once again. The Federal Reserve will try to deliberately reflate by printing large amounts of dollars. The "cure" may work for a while, but there's a good chance that it will fail and that the economy will get worse—while prices begin to go up again and money loses value.

The hunter-warrior attitude is perfect for such a situation. Don't expect national policies to make sense. Give up the currently pervasive belief that the government or some other "Big Brother" is obligated to take care of you. Forget about "Big Brother." Take care of yourself.

Neither inflation nor depression are to be feared. In spite of what you have read or may remember about the Great Depression, the fact is that there were millions of Americans who not only survived, but did reasonably well during the 1930s. Some were simply lucky. Others must have known that the boom would not last forever. A number of great fortunes were begun in those days.

Think like a financial warrior. If the price of your house is high relative to other things and you can find another place to live more cheaply, consider selling it. The hunter-warrior needs a home base, but he is basically nomadic by temperament. He will trade one cave for another, erect a lean-to in a new location. Psychologically—unlike the prevailing attitude of the American middle-class—he does not think of his home as his castle; he feels that his blanket or his sleeping bag is his home.

On the other hand, when the rate of inflation is rising and the currency is depreciating rapidly—so rapidly that money is "free" (interest rates that are lower than the rate of inflation)—you should consider taking out a mortgage or borrowing for some other purpose and let inflation pay off your debts.

In the years ahead, you will probably live in a fundamentally inflationary world—that is, your money will lose value over the long run. But, like the seasons, there will be alternating periods of inflation and deflation. Prices will rise and prices will fall—and not always in the same proportion to each other.

The hunter-warrior does not really care whether the economy is under pressure from inflation or deflation. He concentrates on remaining alert, so he can take advantage of either situation.

For example, the fall in the prices of gold and diamonds —which lost half their value from 1980 through 1982— showed clearly that the flight from paper money into tangibles was replaced by a flight from tangible fads into the much-maligned paper dollar. Suddenly, the prices of things that have been rising for years began to crumble. But as a government creates credit and prints money and the money flows into the economy to trigger a new price inflation, first stocks and then gold, antiques, paintings and jewelry inevitably rise again.

During recessionary periods, you accumulate cash while you wait for opportunities to buy. During this phase, probably the safest place for money is in short-term (less than one year) U.S. Treasury obligations (T-Bills). This is because, barring a revolution, the government is liable to see to it that its short-term debt is serviced promptly and in full. Money market mutual funds that are invested only in U.S. government securities are also secure where funds with commercial paper or unsecured corporate IOUs are not.

You can still use a bank for current money, even during a partial banking collapse. In a real emergency, the banking system probably will be nationalized. The Federal Deposit Insurance Corporation does not have the assets to shore up any more than a handful of insolvent banks, but the Federal Reserve, with its ability to literally create credit and print money in an endless flow, is ready and willing to prevent a serious banking panic at whatever the cost. This underlying fact is what will make it different from the 1930s—an inflationary depression.

The recession of 1974 taught us that you can simultaneously have a high rate of inflation *and* unemployment. While there was much talk of a deflationary collapse, it did not take place as the Federal Reserve pumped billions of dollars into the nation's banking system. We can anticipate a duplication of this pattern again. Under the long wave theory as first articulated by Nikolai D. Kondratieff, the Russian economist who was banished to Siberia for his views, the 1980s will witness an economic breakdown similar to that of the 1930s, ushering in a long period of declining economic activity and declining prices similar to the quarter-century periods following the depressions of 1819 and 1874.

However, under the present financial system, the government can quite literally create a false and temporary prosperity almost at will by creating and spending money. Of course, the boom is disjointed and short-lived. In a matter of months the money creation feeds back into the economy as price inflation, and the benefits of the artificially created purchasing power rapidly begin to disappear. If the unemployment rate has been 15 to 20 percent, the spending programs will probably be able to reduce it to 10 to 15 percent, or even less. The real productivity and purchasing power of the nation will be in decline, but most people will have jobs. They will be taking home less purchasing power; they will have less to spend on luxuries and vacations, but most will be eating. Social and political tensions will be at a high point. Periodic widespread rioting will be almost inevitable, but an ultimate breakdown of law and order is not really likely.

Still, as we indicated in chapter V, there is a possibility that a renewal of inflation may be handled in such a way that it will be relatively painless for most people. There are nations—such as Brazil—that have learned to live with triple-digit inflation over a long period of years. One approach is to index wages and prices to the inflation rate, which means that everyone makes a little more money every month and everything costs a little more at the same time. As long as wages and prices stay in step, the pleasant side of inflation can overwhelm the painful side. But even if all these projections are wrong, and something quite different takes place, as a hunter-warrior, you don't need to be thrown off balance.

The individuals who have built financial liquidity and stored their purchasing power during the deflationary stage of stop-go, will be able to roll with the punches and put their money back into tangibles such as gold and silver, artworks, antiques and real estate when the money supply figures are signaling "go" by expanding corporate and personal financial liquidity.

This basically is the strategy for survival and prosperity during an inflationary depression. There will be a time to buy common stocks and a time to sell them, a time to speculate in commodities, a time to buy tangibles and put them away, and a time to buy only government Treasury bills. Sometimes your timing will be wrong, there will be no real economic security for anyone—but has there ever been? For the hunter-warrior, insecurity is a way of life. He quite literally never knew where his next meal was coming from, but he survived and we have his habits and traditions with us still—buried in the collective unconscious of the race. Thus, in times of insecurity, do not seek security—seek tension, even adventure.

Most Americans are unsophisticated about making money in a declining economy, and are reluctant to go short stocks or buy commodities or put options or sell calls. We are a nation of optimists and some feel it's actually un-American to take money while others are losing their shirts. But as long as markets exist, there is always a winning position. You may be losing but you can be sure that on the other side of the table, someone is making money. Consider the case of the man we ran across in Beirut while heavy fighting was going on a few years ago. This man went around the city buying up choice real estate at bargain prices. Many who knew about it thought he was crazy, but when the fighting wound down a bit, it turned out that the crazy real estate buyer had already more than doubled his money.

The moral is clear: there will always be opportunities. As far as jobs are concerned, the world of stop-go tends to concentrate businesses and create huge corporate and government monoliths. Therefore, it is better to work for a large organization than a small one—as long as you realize that even the largest organization can fail, so that you cultivate a personal attitude of self-reliance for emergencies. But a real economic breakdown will restore the importance of the small business, as it has done in Italy.

If you don't have much capital to preserve, consider learning a new trade, becoming expert at a skill you don't now possess or at least becoming physically fit. Above all, don't become a slave to money. You cannot defeat an enemy you regard as all powerful. Therefore, paradoxically, to make money, you should set goals in your life that go beyond money. This gives you objectivity. To some extent, you should even have contempt for money—particularly fiat money. It is only a medium of exchange—the politician's tranquilizer for the voter. Several years ago I used to get my seminar audience to take a dollar bill and tear it up. Do this and you will experience a strange feeling of relief and freedom. This is because by your action, you symbolically become the master of your money, not its fearful servant.

One of the first attitudes that people face in an economic disaster is the feeling of helplessness, the feeling of being in the grip of events over which they have no control, the fear that somehow the game of life has been rigged and they will never be able to win. It is an insidious and demoralizing idea that has been fostered for years by those who believe in big government. After all, the justification of big government is the thesis that basically man is unable to look out for himself. A million years of history refutes this ridiculous idea.

The trouble is that many people think they have no choice. The division of labor in the family and society and the technological interdependence of our civilization makes us all feel less independent, less able to take care of ourselves in an emergency. And yet, we sell ourselves short in holding such beliefs.

You must get over the idea that you have no power. The hunter-warrior knows he always has inner resources of power. You are not really at the mercy of your boss, your business or the environment. If you think you are, it's simply a habit of mind. Most people find that they can do much more than they thought they could when circumstances forced the need on them.

But let's get back to the direct application of hunter-warrior attitudes. How can you face an environment in which you are not sure how much your money is going to be worth from one year to the next, in which your long-term financial security is in doubt, in which your job may be in jeopardy, in which your physical environment is deteriorating and in which the leadership of your country becomes increasingly less credible?

The credo of the ancient Japanese samurai applies here:

> I have no parents; I make the heavens and the earth my parents.
> I have no home; I make *seika tanden** my home.
> I have no divine power; I make honesty my divine power.
> I have no means; I make docility my means.
> I have no magic power; I make personality my magic power.
> I have neither life nor death; I make A UM my life and death.
> I have no body; I make stoicism my body.
> I have no eyes; I make the flash of lightning my eyes.
> I have no ears; I make sensibility my ears.
> I have no limbs; I make promptitude my limbs.
> I have no laws; I make self-protection my laws.
> I have no strategy; I make "free to kill and free to restore life" my strategy.

---

*Seika tanden is the "one-point in the lower abdomen," just below the navel, considered the body's center of gravity and the center of spiritual energy; the term is in many ways synonymous with Hara.

> I have no designs; I make "taking opportunity by the fore-
> lock" my designs.
> I have no miracles; I make righteous laws my miracles.
> I have no principles; I make adaptability to all circum-
> stances my principles.
> I have no tactics; I make emptiness and fullness my
> tactics.
> I have no talent; I make ready wit my talent.
> I have no friends; I make my mind my friend.
> I have no enemy; I make incautiousness my enemy.
> I have no armor; I make benevolence and righteousness
> my armor.
> I have not castle; I make immovable-mind my castle.
> I have no sword; I make absence-of-mind my sword.

It might be useful for you to repeat these statements to yourself while sitting quietly in a meditative position once a day. Also, as emphasized earlier, any form of personal discipline, physical or mental, is extremely valuable, whether it be a form of physical exercise or refraining from drinking or smoking. Increasingly, medical experts are recognizing that the mind and body are one. I learned in 1978 that a person who can face a strong opponent in a karate class can face a difficult or dangerous market situation without flinching—and make the right decision.

The increased popularity of martial arts in the United States reflects not so much an interest in physical combat, but a search for reestablishment of the mind-body disciplines and mental attitudes of primal man which all the recent evidence shows probably dominated his thinking and outlook for at least 10 million years and which may comprise the core of the modern human personality. We see an increased interest in physical activity in all spheres of daily living, whether it be jogging or running or watching a professional football game on television on Sunday. Charles

Prevish, associate professor of religious studies at Penn State, in fact, believes that sports in America has now taken on the aspect of religion. "It is now rather ordinary," says Prevish:

> to hear about getting it together, feeling complete, peaking, and a host of other equally impressive terms signalling a concern for utilizing sports participation as a means for marshaling some small bit of human wholeness in very troubled times.

"Religion is the means for ultimate transformation and so is sport," continues Prevish, making comparisons between seemingly timeless hours spent in church, synagogue and mosque and the runner's solitary ten-mile jog at dawn.

The foreign exchange trader or specialist on the floor of the New York Stock Exchange experiences the same kind of high or peak experience when, alone, he takes a high-risk trading decision and, like the hunter after the kill, experiences the victory of a winning trade.

Warriors of all cultures and periods of history have attempted to develop a sense of oneness with their universe and a natural response pattern to dangers and challenges to their welfare. There are striking parallels between samurai traditions and warrior traditions of the American Indian. For instance, in *A Separate Reality,* Carlos Castaneda quotes the Indian sorcerer, Don Juan, as follows:

> It is up to us as single individuals to oppose the forces of our lives. I have said this to you countless times: only a warrior can survive. A warrior knows that he is waiting and what he is waiting for; and while he waits he wants nothing and thus whatever little thing he gets is more than he can take. If he needs to eat he finds a way, because he is not hungry; if something hurts his body, he finds a way to stop it, because he is not in pain. To be hungry or to be in pain means that the man has abandoned himself and is no longer a warrior; and the forces of hunger and pain will destroy him.

156

For the modern American, preoccupied with bills and status and family problems, the message is: If you lose your job or your money, don't panic. Keep your cool.

In *Journey to Ixtlan*, Castaneda suggests that the individual take death as his adviser, which strikingly parallels Yamamoto Tsunenori's advice to "choose death." Castaneda says:

> Whenever you feel, as you always do, that everything is going wrong and you're about to be annihilated, turn to your death and ask if that is so. Your death will tell you that you are wrong; that nothing really matters outside of touch, your death will tell you, "I haven't touched you yet."

Our refusal to contemplate death may be at bottom the reason for our apparent refusal to face economic depression or decline. In *The Denial of Death*, Pulitzer prize-winner Ernest Becker forcibly argues that, only by accepting death and not hiding from it, can Western man be liberated from his destructive impulses. Picking up the same theme, the famous Japanese novelist, Yukio Mishima, in *The Way of the Samurai* makes the following comment:

> We do not like to extract from death its beneficial elements and try to put them to work for us. We always try to direct our gaze toward the bright landmark, the forward facing landmark, the landmark of life. And we try our best not to refer to the power by which death gradually eats away our lives. This outlook indicates a process by which our rational humanism, while constantly performing the function of turning the eyes of modern man toward the brightness of freedom and progress, wipes the problem of death from the level of consciousness, pushing it deeper and deeper into the subconscious, turning the death impulse by this repression to an ever more dangerous, explosive, ever more concentrated, inner-directed impulse. We are ignoring the fact that bringing death to the level of consciousness is an important element of mental health.

When looked at in the light of our own individual demise, the fate of our society seems less important and its problems easier to cope with. For, in the final analysis, for you and for me as individuals, there is no difference between an atomic bomb dropped on our city and a fatal heart attack. With this problem out of the way, there is merely the problem of shelter to be found, food to be gathered and cooked, and personal relations with other human beings—in short, the problems of the hunter-warrior.

In this context, trading and investing simply become a more complex methodology of survival, a form of financial jujitsu. Whether facing a human enemy or a wild animal in the woods or a stock market quote tape or Quotron, your prime enemy is fear. Fear confuses the mind and inhibits the natural protective response. Fear inhibits creativity and shuts out the clarity of view necessary to make successful trades and investments. I can speak with authority about this because literally I have made millions when I was able to conquer fear and I have lost equal amounts when I have been blinded by this enemy.

I know human beings and I know that I do not need to elaborate further on this point because we all know in our hearts what we fear and when we fear it, but the prescription for conquering this primary enemy is real, relatively simple to define, but difficult to achieve. And that is, simply to persist in your endeavor despite the fear until the action becomes a habit and the fear disappears, as it will.

The same viewpoint applies regarding our society. All civilizations of the past have eventually come to an end and ours probably will be no exception. But a positive attitude will enable us to make the most of the here and now, whatever it is. And if enough people think this way, Armageddon may be postponed for a hundred years.

Perhaps one of the most perceptive statements of how the seemingly negative idea of death can be used to confront and overcome fear was made by J. Glenn Gray in his little-noted book, *The Warriors: Reflections on Men in Battle*. Philosophizing upon his own direct combat experience in World War II, Gray says:

> As a consequence of temperament and experience, some soldiers can learn to regard death as an anticipated experience among other experiences, something they plan to accept when the time comes for what it is. They take death into life, as it were, and seek to make it a part of experience, sometimes winning thereby an intimate relationship. Because they respect death as a power and do not fear it as a blind fate, they are able to reckon their chances in warfare with greater calmness than other soldiers. For them, death is as much a self-evident fact as birth, and they regard as foolish the man who refuses to accept the one as the other. Since moral or religious considerations hardly occupy first rank with such soldiers, they are unlikely to choose death as a means or an end to self-improvement or atonement. However, the more imaginative and thoughtful of this type do regard death as that absolute in human existence which gives life its poignancy and intensity. *They do not desire to live forever*, for they feel that this would be a sacrifice of quality to gain quantity. In philosophical terms, such soldiers are affirming human finiteness and limitation as a morally desirable fact. Just as the bliss of erotic life is conditioned by its transiency, so life is sweet because of the threats of death that envelop it and in the end swallow it up. Men of this sort are usually in love with life and avid for experience of every sort. . . . Action is their element, and their hearts are in the future as it unfolds itself every day. They look out upon the world as adventure and upon themselves as capable of storming all its ramparts.

How does all of the foregoing apply directly to your behavior regarding trading and investing? Let's translate it into rules that you can use immediately to improve your performance in the world of money:

► 1. *Don't be a half-warrior.* Fight your own battle. To enter a market on your own intuition and then get out when someone offers a differing opinion is like changing weapons in the middle of a fight. Losing concentration and direction, you are bound to lose financially. If you do not want to be a financial warrior, have someone do it for you (an investment advisor). But delegate the responsibility completely by giving him power of attorney to act on your behalf. Let him (or her) be *your* warrior.

► 2. *Know your strengths and weaknesses and use them.* For example, if you know you tend to overtrade, or take too many positions, make a conscious effort not to do this. Resist the feeling that you may miss an opportunity and limit your actions. If your strong point is to spot opportunities ahead of the crowd, do not wait for confirmation from others. Strike out boldly on your own

► 3. *If possible, never let a profit become a loss.* This is particularly true in these uncertain times. Once you have begun to defeat your hidden opponents in the financial markets (be they professional traders or large institutions) press on strongly, but select a point where you will take your profit. Musashi would call this "to crush": "In single combat, if the enemy is less skillful than oneself, if his rhythm is disorganized, or if he has fallen into evasive or retreating attitudes, we must crush him straight-

160

away, with no concern for his presence and without allowing him space for breath."

▶ 4. *Know the general economic condition and always have an overall point of view, even if you subsequently have to change it.* For me, this perhaps has been the most important rule. Without broad convictions, deeply and confidently held, you can be frightened out of an investment or trading position by the slightest rumor. A bear market cannot be reversed by a week-long rally. One good quarterly earnings report may not signal the turnaround of a stock. If the economy is in a depression, it will not pull out overnight. Therefore, look for trading and investment opportunities in the context of the big picture. Concentrate on this first.

As Musashi said: "Perception is broad and sight is weak . . .it is important to see distant things as if they were close and to take a distant view of close things." Since he is not a sight-seer, the successful hunter goes about this task with great concentration. He knows how to follow tracks and signs left by animals and automatically interprets their meaning. He knows how to get information from local inhabitants and how to evaluate it. Sure of his own senses, the hunter knows that information from others is always biased by their outlook and beliefs. In some places, friendly natives will tell him what he wants to hear. In others, they will make up stories to entertain him. The hunter knows that sifting fact from fancy requires thoughtful questioning that will help separate what is really true from mere conjecture and folklore. But his overall gaze should be large and broad.

You face the same problem in the investment jungle. Information comes from many sources and in many forms. You must learn to recognize what is fact and what is opinion, what is true and what might be true, or could be true or isn't true. Some of the information comes to you as statistics and announcements from the Federal Reserve, the patterns on charts, the ebb and flow of numbers, the empty store windows in a neighborhood, and the price of used yachts. Much of your information comes from other inhabitants of the jungle in the form of news, gossip and so-called inside information, but the best information comes from the "void." That is, after you have gathered all the facts, it comes from your feelings and intuition.

Selecting what you need from a flood of data requires a skeptical attitude. Bismarck once said, "Nothing is confirmed until officially denied." So you should not believe everything you hear or read, particularly from politicians in government. One of the best ways to separate truth from falsehood is to ask the basic question of a famous French detective: "Who benefits financially?" If an oil executive warns of an oil shortage, it is obvious that the oil companies will benefit from higher oil prices. Therefore, the statement should be treated skeptically. Yet, you can't be too skeptical. Remember the world is always changing, so you should keep your mind open to new ideas, even if, at first, they seem strange or outlandish.

▶ 5. *Use market judo.* One of the principles of the Asian martial arts is to let the enemy's own strength defeat him. This is a key technique in judo. Instead of resisting a rushing attack, you give way before it and attempt to turn its force to your advantage. Exactly the same technique can be applied in trading and investing. Say you are bullish in some particular stock or commodity and inexplicably it turns viciously against you. Instead of holding on to your position, you give way and sell out. Not only that, you sell short, in effect, using the force of the market itself to earn profits for you. In practice, this is extremely difficult to do. To reverse a well-thought-out position is an anathema even to some professional traders. But if you can learn how to do this, you will have added a powerful weapon to your financial survival arsenal. Put simply, it is easier to ride the horse in the direction it is going. So if the market turns on you, turn with it.

▶ 6. *Have a talisman.* Throughout the ages warriors have adopted a particular mode of dress and carried some physical object that symbolized their belief in themselves or their cause. For the Crusades, it was the cross; for the Prussian cavalry in Wellington's army at Waterloo, it was the death's head; for GIs in World War II, it was a Bible, a lucky charm, or an extra weapon. Whether you carry it or put it on your desk in your office or home, you should have some sort of talisman, or good luck charm. It is *not* silly or superstitious. It gives you something on which to concentrate for purposes of meditation, and to symbolize your attitude. For example, when I was making enormous trading profits in the Japanese yen, I had a wall hanging with a fierce drawing of a Japanese samurai warrior just above my Reuters TV monitor of the currency interbank markets. On another occasion, I was wearing a belt with an eagle buckle when I was winning one day and so I kept on wearing it, even though it was uncomfortable, for weeks—until it ceased to work as a lucky charm. The moral here is to use or wear whatever gives you confidence in your fight for financial survival.

▶ 7. *The war cry.* Karate teaches you to shout when you attack. This tightens your muscles and, sometimes, throws your adversary completely off balance. More importantly, it gives tangible expression to and dramatizes your confident, aggressive feelings. That is why since ancient times warriors have had war cries and battle songs. I once knew an extremely successful entrepreneur who used to play Khachaturian's "Sabre Dance" as he drove to work to get him in the mood for the day. You may not want to shout a war cry to your broker, but expressing some form of symbolic physical aggression, even as simple a thing as pounding a desk with a rolled up magazine, or even your fist, will reinforce your ability to follow the way of the hunter-warrior in transactions which you may have thought of until now as purely mental.

▶ 8. *Have reserve power.* In almost every battle in history, experienced generals have always known to keep some of their forces in reserve—not to put the entire outcome on one roll of the dice unless there is no other choice. By the same token, in trading particularly, you should have reserve financial ammunition to back up your margin position if it should go against you. This also makes it less necessary that your timing be perfect, and at worst, if you lose, you can live financially to fight another day. However, if you are on "death ground" financially with no sure certainty of a second chance, do not be afraid to use all the financial resources at your command.

▶ 9. *Go for the killing.* Many people waste countless hours and days on trading or investment positions that are too small relative to their income and life style. How many times have you heard someone brag that he doubled his investment, or made two or three times the amount he put into a stock. Then comes the inevitable question: How many shares did you have? Unless you are learning or practicing, you should always have positions that would make a difference in your financial life. Otherwise, conserve your energies and become a spectator. Very few people ever made a killing without taking up the long sword of risk.

A killing is a natural consequence of your focused act. As Musashi might explain it, your intention is to cut—not slash—the enemy decisively. In other words to make a killing is your natural goal. On the other hand, a financial warrior never holds onto a losing position to prove his courage—only to eventually win. This is his overriding intention and the true meaning of *Ai Uchi!*

With the hunter-warrior attitude, you will be in touch with the predominant tradition of mankind over the greatest extent of its history. Know that you are a hunter-warrior on potentially hostile terrain; that you want mainly what you need to survive and that you can make even the most seemingly alien country work for you. You need friends, opportunities and good luck. But know that you can accept the possibility of financial failure; that you can accept material gain or loss with equanimity. Also know that you are dedicated to the preservation of mankind and to the health of the planet. This is the way of the hunter-warrior.

If you can adhere to this stance in trading and investing, you not only will be able to cope with the difficult economic conditions ahead, but you may even become rich. More importantly, you will have achieved inner calm and peace of mind knowing that, whatever happens, your life will be happier and more satisfying because you have followed the way of courage and decision—the way of the hunter-warrior.